THE
Archive Photographs
SERIES

DONNINGTON
AND MUXTON

With best wishes from the Author,

Allan Frost

September 1983: the first of two great fires at the Central Ordnance Depot, Donnington, which not only caused some £150 million of damage but also led to public health fears through widespread asbestos fall-out. Photograph courtesy of the Editor, Shropshire Star.

THE
Archive Photographs
SERIES

DONNINGTON AND MUXTON

Compiled by
Allan Frost

To my daughter Caroline, as a reminder of where she grew up

TEMPUS

Tempus Publishing Limited
The Mill, Brimscombe Port,
Stroud, Gloucestershire, GL5 2QG

ISBN 0 7524 2250 2

Typesetting and origination by
Tempus Publishing Limited
Printed in Great Britain by
Midway Colour Print, Wiltshire

Extract from William Hole's map of Shropshire, c. 1610. Donnington is named Dunnyton, adjacent to Kinges Wood, the remnants of the ancient Royal Forest (which, in Medieval times, extended to the Wrekin Hill). The fact that this was a deer park and hence out of bounds to ordinary folk is symbolised by a fence drawn inside part of the wood, although no actual fence may have existed.

Contents

Acknowledgements

Many people and organisations have contributed information and illustrations for this book, including L. Aldred, P. Ashley, K. Beddowes, J. Bray, C. Brown, I. Brown, R. Camp, D. Coxill, Donnington Wood Baptist church, M. Finch, A. Fisher, C. Fletcher, P. Frost, G. Gaut, GenFind (Telford) Ltd, S. Growcott, D. Hobson, Ironbridge Gorge Museum, S. King, S. & M. Kirkpatrick, C. Lake, W. & K. Lawrence, R. Lembicz, P. Luter, F. & N. Mansell, B. Mapp, M. Millward, S. Onions, M. Phillips, R. Price, A. Rigby, D. Ryder, M. Seaman, C. Shaw, Shrewsbury Records & Research Library, *Shropshire Star*, G. Smith, Y. Taylor, J. Wall and Wellington Library. I am very grateful to them all and apologise sincerely to anyone who has been inadvertently omitted. Thanks are also due to my wife Dorothy for her help and support.

St Matthew's church and The Common, 1979. Queens Road lies across the top of the photograph and St Matthew's National School (demolished in the 1990s) is situated above the church.

Introduction

I published a booklet called *The Story of Donnington and its Parish Church* in 1979 as my first venture into writing a local history. Now, over twenty years later and after many requests to 'do it again', I am pleased this book is now ready for publication. More to the point, it contains many illustrations hitherto unpublished and much more information.

Until some 250 years ago, the history of this part of Shropshire was almost inextricably linked to that of nearby Lilleshall. Consequently, I have included detail which, on the face of it, has little to do with the boundaries of modern Donnington or Muxton.

However, Donnington previously included portions of land in what are now the parishes of St Georges and Wrockwardine Wood; I have endeavoured to include information concerning those areas where appropriate to the overall story. It must be remembered that modern Donnington strictly comprises three separate settlements: 'old' Donnington grew up along the old Wellington-Newport main road; Donnington Wood originated as part of an ancient Royal forest; New Donnington was created shortly before the outbreak of the Second World War.

In a similar way, although Muxton has been virtually insignificant throughout its history and straddles the Donnington-Lilleshall parish boundary (marked by a stream to the west of the White House Hotel), it is included because it lies within the general area covered by this history.

I lived in Donnington Wood for over 15 years and throughout my life have never lived more than five miles away from it. Like many of the indigenous population, I have long been irritated by too much attention being paid to the Ironbridge area, particularly since the history of other parts of what is now Telford have equally fascinating and arguably longer histories. I hope this book goes some way to proving the point.

As far as illustrations are concerned, I have tried to limit them to buildings which have been demolished or altered significantly and events which are relevant to paint a picture of life in this area. There seems little point in including pictures of places extant and unchanged, although in fact there are precious few of them left.

I have endeavoured to include everything relevant to the events which made Donnington, Donnington Wood and Muxton what they are today. However, I am bound to have omitted something; no one can know everything. I have particularly made a point of not dwelling on the events of the past twenty years or so, for the simple reason that it is difficult to be objective when events are current. A good historian should let the dust settle before drawing conclusions, although some comments are warranted. Anyway, twenty years is no time at all in a story which covers thousands.

As you will see…

Allan Frost
July 2001

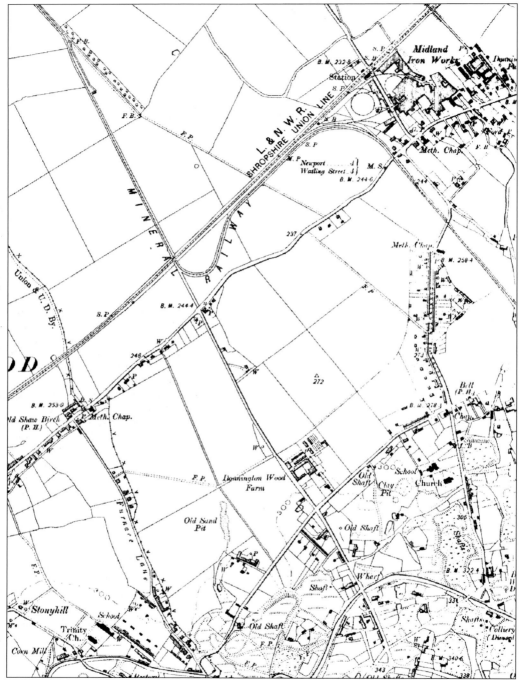

Donnington and Donnington Wood: detail from 1903 Ordnance Survey map. All of the central and northern farmland is now occupied by New Donnington and the Central Ordnance Depot. Neither the railway lines nor the Donnington Wood Canal now exist. The Midland Iron Works was demolished in the 1990s to make way for new road layouts and housing.

One

Beginnings

Very little can be said, with certainty, regarding the early occupation of the Donnington Wood area, prior to the Norman invasion in 1066. The name 'Donnington' may be derived from 'Dunn' or 'Dunning', the name of a Saxon, probably the head of a settlement, and 'tun', the old English word for a farm.

Alternatively, it may be that the name of the settlement was simply 'the place by the hill', which is what the Saxon word 'dunning' actually meant. If so, then the hill referred to could have been Lilleshall Hill since it is the only one of any visual distinction in the area. In any event, the location of the farm is not known but may well have been on a site near Donnington Farm, situated close to an ancient trackway, now followed by the former main Wellington to Newport road.

The development of this area of east Shropshire has been strongly influenced by varied climactic conditions over millennia. In particular, the shallow warm and clear seas of the Lower Carboniferous geological period deposited limestone in the Lilleshall area. Subsequent cyclical sedimentation in the deltas of the Upper Carboniferous Period deposited coal, clay and iron ore at Donnington Wood, features which contributed so much to the early stages of the Industrial Revolution during the eighteenth century.

Earth movements in later geological periods resulted in severe faulting, helping to expose the coal and iron ore and thus promote early mining activities in the area. However, they also caused immense extraction difficulties in the late twentieth century, ultimately leading to the closure of the mines on economic grounds.

Some of the most significant periods in more recent geological history were the successive Ice Ages. Shropshire was engulfed by the slow moving but extensive effects of compacted ice from not only the mountainous parts of Wales but also by glaciers from as far away as the Lake District. Before the Ice Ages, the River Severn flowed northwards, joining the sea at the estuary of the present River Dee. The extremely low temperatures of the Ice Ages froze virtually all surface water and only permitted rivers to flow beneath the ice.

Eventually, 15,000 years ago, overall temperatures began to rise again, the ice began to melt and the Severn resumed its flow. However, the retreat of ice from north Wales and the Irish Sea was slow and the waters of the river built up into lakes which eventually linked up and whose shores reached Wenlock Edge and the higher ground in southern Donnington.

The greatest of these lakes was named Lake Lapworth after the geologist who first postulated its existence. It was of major significance to the subsequent human history of east Shropshire because it eventually overflowed at Ironbridge, where the speed of water and the glacial debris it carried gouged out a new course for the river to follow. After the glaciers disappeared the previous channel northwards was blocked by moraines; thus the River Severn continues to flow southwards into the Bristol Channel.

The draining of Lake Lapworth left behind substantial deposits of fluvial sand and gravel and helped to shape the countryside, improving drainage and soil structure in some areas and enhancing its subsequent suitability for arable farming.

It was during the latter stages of the last Ice Age that animals and man took up residence in central and eastern Shropshire. Among the most notable of the creatures which moved into the area were mammoths; evidence of them was found at Condover, near Shrewsbury, in 1986. Several mammoth skeletons, both adult and young, were discovered in what was once a large mud-bottomed kettle hole left behind by the glaciers some 12,700 years ago. These mammoths appear to have ventured into the depression in search of food and become stuck fast; their desperate efforts to extricate themselves were in vain.

Mammoths are believed to have been a nomadic species who wandered in search of adequate feeding grounds. Wherever they travelled they were closely followed by early man who, with his primitive weapons, risked his life to slay these monstrous creatures (one of the male skeletons discovered at Condover was almost four metres tall) in order to eat the meat, use the fur for clothing and the tusks for weapons and implements.

Man first occupied parts of Britain when it was connected to the European continent. These first inhabitants were the Neoliths – so named because their weapons and utensils were fashioned from stone. They were short, dark haired, swarthy folk who survived by hunting wild animals. The Neoliths were followed by Celtic (or Gallic) races who had discovered how to make bronze artefacts from copper and tin; they were characterised as being taller, heavier and fair haired and arrived in Britain after it had become an island.

The Celts lived on hill tops fortified with ramparts of earth or stone within which they constructed circular huts with roofs made from branches covered with sods of earth and grass.

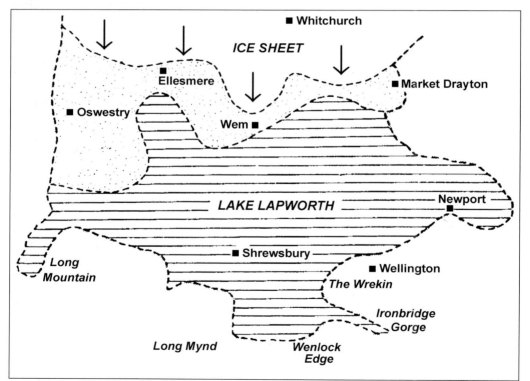

Lake Lapworth: plan showing the identifiable extent of this Ice Age lake. The waters broke and formed the Ironbridge Gorge. Thereafter, the course of the River Severn ran southwards; it had previously flowed northwards.

The hill fort atop the Wrekin Hill, some five miles south west of Donnington, is an excellent example of a Celtic hill fort, which not only gave the necessary protection from wild animals and human enemies but also afforded extensive views in all directions. It became the regional capital of the tribe known by the Romans as the Cornovii.

Although Julius Caesar made two very brief visits to Britain (in 55 BC and the following year), his army only ventured a few miles inland. The invasion by Roman legions actually began a century later in AD 43 when Claudius was emperor. The Romans knew that effective lines of supply and communication were vital if they were to stand any real chance of success and consolidation, even with their iron weaponry and daunting armour. To this end they concentrated on building a comprehensive road system which enabled legionnaires to move swiftly from one area of conflict to another. At relatively regular intervals along each road they constructed rectangular-shaped camps occupied by small garrisons of soldiers to act as local peace-keeping forces and to protect the highway.

One such camp was Uxacona, situated on what is now known as Red Hill, just north of Watling Street near the remnants of Grange Colliery (there is also evidence there of an earlier Iron Age settlement). Part of the site is now occupied by a reservoir. This stretch of Watling Street, previously an ancient trackway, formed part of the Roman road between Letocetum (now named Wall in Staffordshire) and Uriconium (Wroxeter) near Atcham. Uriconium began life as the headquarters of the 14th ('Gemina') Legion between AD 50 and 70 and, after a few years of occupation when the threat of local revolt had practically disappeared, developed into the fifth largest Roman city in Britain. The site at Uxacona indicates that it was developed and reshaped by the Romans several times during their occupation.

Many of the Cornovii who survived the invasion left the Wrekin hilltop and eventually settled in prosperous Uriconium on the banks of the Severn, upon which river they manoeuvred their traditional coracle boats with expertise.

The Romans remained in Britain, enjoying a long period of relatively peaceful coexistence with the indigenous population. They departed at the end of the fourth century. Within this period of time many of the soldiers and their auxiliaries married local people and settled down in their own farmstead villas, usually not too distant from the safety of one of the towns or camps. The greater part of Shropshire was under woodland and forest, a landscape which afforded little protection from wild animals and outlaws. It made survival sense to stay close to one's friends and supporters.

The Saxon, Angle and Jute attacks on Britain began during the final years of Roman occupation. Uriconium was destroyed by the former towards the end of the sixth century. These piratical tribes from northern Europe had been invited into the country as mercenaries and later rebelled, initially colonising eastern counties before progressively advancing westwards; the Jutes in Kent, the Saxons in the north and central regions and the Angles in the south.

Eastern Shropshire formed part of the Saxon kingdom of Mercia, named after the Saxon word 'mark', or border, because it was adjacent to the Marches or borderlands of Wales which remained occupied by Celtic tribes. For several centuries Saxon Britain was torn by war, not only against the Welsh but also between the leaders of the various Anglo-Saxon kingdoms.

By the seventh century Shropshire was divided into two Mercian Provinces: Magonsaete held the land to the south of the River Severn; Wreocansaete ('settlers around the Wrekin') belonged to a separate tribe who held the land north of the river. The land upon which Donnington lies was in the latter province. Offa, the Mercian king most memorable for the erection of the lengthy earthwork or dyke which bears his name, is credited with having both the power and diplomatic skills to make a pact with the Welsh to define a clear boundary between his lands and theirs. The dyke provided some degree of security to both sides and helped to consolidate Offa's lands in Shropshire.

As time progressed, farming communities appeared in places previously considered inhospitable; it was then that the unique system of strip farming, which was to characterise the English landscape for several centuries, developed. Christianity began to take root and Anglo-

Saxon churches appeared as focal points for the new villages and hamlets populated by increasing immigration. It is believed that the present stone church at Lilleshall, dating from King Stephen's reign in the twelfth century, was built on the site of a wooden Saxon building, probably erected in the seventh century.

The Saxons also introduced a new system of government and divided their kingdoms (eventually dominated by the Kingdom of Wessex, later ruled by King Alfred) into Shires. Each Shire was subdivided into Hundreds; each Hundred held its own court to mete out justice and fell within the jurisdiction of a local earl; serious offences were referred to the Shire or County Court. Donnington fell within the boundaries of the Wrockwardine ('Recordin') Hundred. The size of these 'Hundreds' varied considerably; tradition has it that a Hundred was an area of land containing one hundred families or dwellings.

Many of the place names in Shropshire changed their original Celtic names to Saxon; for example, Pengwern became Shrewsbury ('Scrobbesbyrig' – 'fort in the scrub'). Settlement names were often based on a Saxon name, appended with variations of such words as bury, burgh, ton, ham and lea. Donnington was one of these settlements.

Unfortunately, apart from some church structures, Saxons made their homes from timber and so far no remains have been discovered in this part of Shropshire, although their occupation is obvious simply because of the characteristic place names bequeathed to later generations.

The Saxons were instrumental in the introduction of ecclesiastical as well as secular boundaries and it is because of this that Donnington was to be associated with Lilleshall for more than a thousand years. Archbishop Theodore, who died in 690, began a process of dividing the whole country into parishes. Lilleshall happened to be the parish into which the Donnington area fell.

The parish stretched from the Weald ('wild') Moors in the north to Watling Street in the south, and from what is now Wrockwardine Wood in the west to Lizard Hill near Shifnal in the east. The original wooden Saxon church at Lilleshall was the centre of ecclesiastical influence once the parish had been created and a priest had been appointed.

It is a fair assumption that the settlement at Donnington was founded during the later period of Saxon dominance when England was united under Wessex domination following the expulsion of the Vikings and it was no longer unsafe to erect homesteads on land cleared for habitation and cultivation in remote forrested areas.

Donnington, the 'farm in the place by the hill', 'Dunn's farm' or 'Dunning's farm' would have provided a source of livelihood and mutual protection for several Saxon households.

The foundations of today's settlement had been laid.

Two

Domesday

Perhaps the most notable year in English history, 1066, saw the end of Saxon rule and the beginning of a long line of Norman and Plantagenet kings. Contrary to popular belief, the Normans were not Frenchmen, nor did they simply embark on the invasion of England purely to subdue the Anglo-Saxon community. They were descended from Norsemen; Vikings who terrorised western Europe between 800 and 1100 and penetrated parts of the Mediterranean, Russia, the Middle East and even Canada. In Britain they were almost constantly in conflict with the Saxon kings and had managed to consolidate their rule ('Danelaw') in eastern parts of the country.

In France, the Norsemen became known as Normans ('men from the north') and ruled over the lands they had taken during the tenth century. By marrying with members of the French nobility they managed to retain their Duchy, ostensibly to provide support for the French kings. By the eleventh century the Normans had become more French than Norse in their way of life.

They were desperate to acquire wealth and power and developed prowess in battle in order to achieve those aims. They were also highly proficient in managing their lands. The fact that their inheritance customs only permitted the eldest son to benefit from a father's death ('primogeniture') meant that younger brothers had to find new estates for themselves. Those lands in England not already under Danelaw were a tempting prospect. One factor which increased the likelihood of military success was that the Normans were skilled in the art of fighting on horseback; the Saxons were not.

In 1066 England was at war with itself. The people in the north were always ready to fight against an English king in the south. Owing to a family connection between the Saxon king, Ethelred, and the Norse Canute, the question of who had the right to the English throne became hotly disputed during the middle of the eleventh century.

The dispute reached a climax in 1066 when Duke William of Normandy, an illegitimate descendant of Edward the Confessor, maintained that his claim was stronger than that of the newly elected King Harold. In fact, this contention was little more than an excuse to invade a country which promised rich pickings for a land- and power-hungry duke. William joined battle with Harold's army and, with fresher and more numerous men, won the day (14th October) by deploying his skilled professionals against Harold's rather disorganised defenders. Normans referred to the Battle of Hastings as the Battle of Senlac ('Lake of Blood').

William then set about the task of consolidating his new possessions. To do this he decreed that all the land in England belonged to him and him alone. Land occupied by anyone else was deemed to be held in custodial control on his behalf, in return for certain services.

Initially he gave estates and positions of power to those who had served him during the Conquest, thus displacing the majority of English Earls. He allowed his supporters to build strongholds in the form of castles near or in the main centres of population (which often meant clearing away dwellings to provide open spaces – 'wastes' – around the castle walls). They were also able to maintain their own company of soldiers to keep the peace locally and to give assistance to William when needed to subdue rebellions. Shrewsbury Castle was built by Roger de Montgomery, a kinsman of William, who had provided part of the fleet that carried the invading army over the Channel as well as some of his own troops.

The Normans excelled in creating legislation and built on existing Anglo-Saxon traditions to enforce their rule. The Shire and Hundred Courts sought not only to protect the positions of the new Baronial Lords but also to impose a greater degree of of law and order. Everyone had rights, including the Saxon Earls, free men and serfs. They were all afforded the protection of their Norman Lord in exchange for services, usually in the form of labour, provisions or taxes.

The effects of Norman rule and their 'feudal' system of land and social management took many years to establish. One major problem William faced was knowing just how extensive and wealthy the lands were that he now ruled.

He therefore appointed a group of Commissioners to visit every part of the country in order to compile a comprehensive inventory of all lands held (or in dispute), together with a breakdown of their population and livestock. The survey (with much inaccurate information) was The Domesday Book, so called by the over-taxed English because there would probably be no equivalent far-reaching reckoning until the Day of Judgement.

The Commissioners wrote down evidence taken from village elders at the Shire and Hundred Courts. Their findings were recorded and constituted, in theory at least, a comprehensive inventory of the size and worth of every manor. Furthermore, they were invaluable in determining the rights by which all individuals held their lands. More to the point, they provided William (and his successors) with a useful source of information upon which levels of taxation and feudal obligation could be set.

The Domesday Book shows that the lands around Lilleshall were held by the church of St Alkmund at Shrewsbury. After the Conquest, when William assumed the patronage of this royal foundation, he gave the estate to Earl Roger de Montgomery who in turn gave it to one of his three learned clerks, Godbold the priest, who already owned a considerable amount of land elsewhere.

The book confirms that the manor of Lilleshall (or, more accurately, Lilleshill or Lilleston) was, at this time, still in the Wrockwardine Hundred and that it possessed ten hides of approximately 120 acres each. (A hide was a vague term used to describe the amount of land under cultivation. In some parts of the country a hide was only 40 or 50 acres in size.)

The precise location of the manor of Lilleshall is uncertain but is generally believed to have been at Ydeshall (Idsall), near Shifnal and, if this was the case, could account for several occasions during the Middle Ages when ownership of land was disputed by the canons at Lilleshall Abbey and the Lords of Ydeshall Manor.

Lilleshall Manor had two ploughs reserved for the lord's own use, ten villagers, five smallholders and three Frenchmen (probably faithful retainers of Godbold) who had another eight ploughs between them, with a further nine possible ploughs to call upon. The fact that the lord had more ploughs than the tenants could support may mean that he was an absentee landlord, who left the village community very much to itself.

The Lilleshall of 1086 also had a mill (possibly at The Humbers) which appears not to have yielded any income for the lord (it may have belonged to the parish church) and one league of woodland. As with the hide measurement, a league was a vague term; it may have covered an area of approximately one square mile. Before the Conquest, the estates at Lilleshall, which would have included the settlement at Donnington, were valued at £6 a year, but at the time of the survey its value had fallen to £4.

Several points of interest arise. No animals are specifically mentioned as belonging to the estate and the number of ploughs seems excessive given the number of inhabitants and the limited amount of cultivated land. Presumably the estate had seen a downturn in its fortunes since the Conquest and there were now fewer inhabitants than before. It is also probable that the smallholders, who were sometimes called 'oxmen', did in fact possess several oxen to pull the ploughs but these were omitted from the survey for some unknown reason.

It is important to remember that the Domesday survey, which was completed in a remarkably short eight months, took no account of ordinary folk like serfs, women and children. Nor did it take into account sources of income which were the sole entitlement of the Church as opposed to the Crown. Its main purpose was to assess tax capabilities for the king's coffers.

Furthermore, the area around Donnington Wood formed part of the extensive Wrekin Royal Forest, also known as the Forest of Mount Gilbert and, later, as Kinge's Wood. It is reasonable to suppose that only a small area of woodland was initially included in Godbold's Lilleshall estate, perhaps the area of ancient forest later known as Abbey Wood.

Unlikely as it may seem, Donnington may have been so small a settlement that it was overlooked in the survey or was included in the overall records for Lilleshall itself. There is a third possibility; that the original wooden Saxon settlement had ceased to exist. However, this is improbable; the name of the settlement is undoubtedly Saxon in origin and any later settlement on this site would not have been given a Saxon name.

The Domesday Book not only allowed the king to realise the extent of his domain; it also stabilised the previously uncertain position regarding land ownership (even though the king technically 'owned' it all) and provided a baseline from which landholders could begin to improve estate management – and thus increase their wealth.

The Medieval Lilleshall estate included almost all the ancient woodland in the parish, much of which was later deemed to be parkland. In 1280, long after the abbey had been built, the abbots received a licence from the king confirming their right to assart (enclose) these woods.

Willmore Grange was one of four granges in Shropshire known to have been owned by the abbey during the Middle Ages. Perhaps of greatest interest was the Watling Street Grange, situated a few metres away from the Roman camp site at Uxacona. It was unusual in that it had a moat, a rare occurrence for a grange farm. Whether the moat was for defensive purposes or merely to separate livestock from the grange buildings is not recorded. Medieval granges were essentially associated with provision of storage for corn, in this case probably for the Abbey. Watling Street Grange is mentioned in the Forest Perambulation

Watling Street Grange, c. 1910.

of 1300 and again in the Excheater Inquisition of 1353, but there is no record of when it ceased to be a working grange. It may have been abandoned during the economic recessions of the late fourteenth century and is not mentioned again until 1551. Excavations of the moat during 1958 failed to find any evidence of Medieval or earlier occupation (which tends to refute arguments that it may have originated as a Roman villa) and it is possible that it was simply an enclosure for livestock.

In 1551 the farm was owned by William Cleobury of Shifnal and leased to successive tenants. The Leveson family acquired it by 1586 and retained ownership until the Duke of Sutherland Lilleshall Estate sales during the First World War, when, in 1917, it was bought by the Ward family. The earliest building structures within the moat perimeter date from the sixteenth century. From about 1670 to 1820 it was occupied by the Dawes family; in 1692 William Dawes died leaving a herd of forty-one cattle, six horses and a large quantity of grain in the barn. His estate was worth a substantial £141. Benjamin Dawes, possibly the last in the family to hold the tenancy, died, aged eighty-one, on 11 April 1840. A field called Dawes Bower, a few hundred metres north of the grange, preserves the family connection.

The present farm buildings appear to have been erected outside the moat during the first two decades of the nineteenth century. The moat was filled and levelled in 1958 by Mr B.J. Ward.

Sketches of Lilleshall Abbey ruins and an Augustinian canon from Charles Walker's A Brief History of Lilleshall, *1891.*

16

Three

Abbey Rule

There were considerable improvements in the way estate management was documented from the time when the Domesday Book was compiled to the end of the thirteenth century. Donnington was mentioned as 'Dunington' in 1145. Various spellings of the name have since arisen: Dunniton (1180 in the Forest Roll); Duninton (1200); Dunyton (1256 in the Assize Court); Donynton and Donyton (1286). Variations in spelling were probably due to scribes who wrote down what they thought they heard; much would depend on the pronunciation of the people speaking to them, and very few could read and write. The same applied to Lilleshall which, even as late as the seventeenth century, was referred to as Linsel, Lindsal and other variants.

It is not certain when the present version of the name became the accepted norm but it was probably during the eighteenth century when literacy became more widespread and map making more prolific. What does seem certain is that its omission from the Domesday Book is more a matter of the Commissioners overlooking individual farmsteads as being unimportant to the task in hand rather than denying their existence.

There can be little doubt that Godbold intended to revitalise his Lilleshall estate in order to increase his wealth and improve his standard of living. Unfortunately he died before he was able to do so and entitlement to the estate passed firstly to his illegitimate son Robert, then to Richard de Belmeis, Bishop of London, who was Viceroy of Shropshire after 1102.

The lands then passed to Richard's nephew, also named Richard de Belmeis (sometimes known as Beaumais or Bellesme), Dean of St Alkmund's, who already held land at Tong in east Shropshire and at Dorchester-on-Thames, where he permitted a small contingent of canons from Arras in Normandy to settle. Several of the new religious orders evolving at this time sought to colonise remote sites. The Arrouasians belonged to the Augustinian Order and sought to live in poverty, celibacy and obedience in accordance with the tenets of St Augustine (Austin) of Hippo who had died in 430.

Richard secured the prebends of the Lilleshall estate and, at the request of his brother Philip de Belmeis, invited the canons to found an abbey there. Some time between 1145 and 1147 the Bishop of Chester received confirmation from the Pope that the endowment was in order, whereupon Richard ceded all his lands in the Lilleshall area to the Arrouasian canons.

The canons occupied land temporarily at Lizard Hill, near Shifnal, then in Donnington Wood for a short time before moving, probably in 1148, to the site where Lilleshall Abbey now stands. Although initially a timber building, the canons began work almost immediately to erect an abbey using local sandstone, the ruins of which may still be seen. They exercised both ecclesiastical and secular control over Donnington Wood for the next 400 years.

The canons were instrumental in the development of both arable and pastoral farming in the area which was then largely forest and rough ground, with a few small farmsteads leased from the abbey. In some respects the open land was more suitable for sheep than humans and the woodland provided good hunting for successive abbots and their guests. It was during the early Middle Ages that part of the Donnington Wood was designated a Deer Park.

The abbey provided services essential to the local population. In addition to normal religious expectations (worship, marriages and burials, etc.), the canons and their many servants treated ailments, including leprosy (a disease spread by Crusaders returning from the wars against the Infidel), provided shelter for the homeless and travelling nobility, and granted pensions to individuals in need. The abbey was a vital institution for the community.

Unfortunately, the Abbey did not own all the land within its boundaries; secular lords held pockets of varying size. This fact complicated the situation and led to many disputes. Minor incursions into the royal forest to bring more land under cultivation were not always executed with prior permission; in 1180 the canons were fined for clearing 7 acres of forest for wheat and 7 acres for oats and some of their tenants in Donnington were fined for similar offences. During the same year Morinus was charged one shilling for a mill in Donnington Wood.

On 13 October 1200, Geoffrey Chanterell sued Walter, Abbot of Lilleshall, at court in Westminster over the right to farm one virgate (about 30 acres) in Donnington after the death of one of his ancestors who had previously held the right. The plaintiff was allowed to keep the land for an annual payment to the abbey of four shillings.

In 1221 the abbots of Shrewsbury and Lilleshall met to resolve a boundary dispute between their respective moorland at Donnington and Kinnersley.

By 1240, the abbot at Lilleshall had obtained the right of Free Warren – permission to hunt over rough ground and woodland owned by the abbey. King Henry III was subsequently entertained twice by the abbot in hunts around Donnington and Lilleshall. Donnington and Lilleshall ('Abbey') Woods were jointly regarded as a Deer Park and, as such, subject to laws strictly governing their use and development. It was probably within Donnington Wood (sometimes called a 'foreign' wood because it lay some distance away from the abbey) where Walter de Dunstanville, the Lord of Shifnal, was granted pannage to feed up to sixty swine.

In 1250 the abbey was permitted to maintain an unauthorised assart (woodland cleared for the purpose of arable farming) of 23 acres in Lilleshall Wood on payment of an annual rent to the Crown.

Schemes for agricultural improvement often involved negotiations with other landowners. The general plan seems to have been to consolidate those pockets of land which fell within the overall boundaries of the Lilleshall estate. Limited success was achieved by exchanging ownership of plots or the granting of certain rights. For example, in 1275, Lord John of Grindle ceded his common rights to the woods on the Lilleshall side of Watling Street.

In 1277 Adam and Ralph of Preston and Robert of Ford ceded their rights of common pasture on all lands enclosed by the abbey within the manor of Lilleshall and at the same time they and Peter of Eyton acknowledged the abbot's right to enclose and reclaim thirty acres of woodland in Donnington Wood, between Waxhillgate and Qualmesmytthe (near Quam Pool), then southwards to the boundary of the old Saxon parish at Watling Street and along Watling Street eastwards to Willmore Grange.

In 1279 Hugh of Haughton ceded his claims to pasture in any part of their lands that had been or were intended for improvement. In the following year Hugh purchased the right to common pasture (excluding horses and goats) in the foreign wood at Donnington together with pannage for twenty-nine pigs and boar between Michaelmas and Martinmas.

There is no doubt that upon the arrival of the canons in Lilleshall there was already a settlement around the Saxon parish church. As was common in these times, disputes over land and rent entitlements were to be expected. After many years of conflict, on 5 March 1286, Bishop Roger de Molend decreed a fixed portion of land for the vicar of the parish church; he was to have the manse, garden, a croft called The Rudyng and an adjoining meadow. In addition, the vicar was to receive the tithes from a variety of farmsteads and woodland, including the hay-tithes of Donnington. This did not prevent successive abbots from extending the size of their holdings. The abbey was able to increase its wealth by levying fines at its court and by taking advantage of secular as well as ecclesiastical laws and customs.

For example, the court was able to assume ownership of land within its boundaries if the previous owner died without leaving an heir. It could also charge for exercising custodial control over an inheritance until a beneficiary came of age. Furthermore, it was common for small gifts of both land and money to be given to the abbey in return for prayers and masses being said upon the death of the donor or a donor's relative, and even for benefactors to pay in advance to ensure burial within the abbey itself.

There can be little doubt that the canons at Lilleshall enjoyed a comfortable lifestyle for many years and perhaps lost sight of the original beliefs upon which their Order was founded. There is evidence that a breakdown of religious life occurred very early in the history of the abbey, when William, the first abbot, became senile and incompetent and let the canons to do whatever they wished.

There was also much criticism of their hunting pleasures in the mid-thirteenth century; perhaps the most telling misdemeanours occurred shortly before the dissolution of the abbey when, in 1519, Abbot John Cockerell was forced to resign his position after only one year because he took pleasure in mixing with women of ill repute. His successor, Robert Watson, the last abbot at Lilleshall, tried his utmost to improve the Abbey's tainted reputation and its poor financial state. He had inherited debts amounting to some 1,000 marks (£600); the abbey's annual income was only £400. By 1525 the debts had been reduced to £370 after much hardship.

For the first two centuries of their occupation of the abbey, the canons enjoyed the relatively secure support of successive monarchs. Even in the troubled times of Stephen's and Matilda's opposing claims to the English throne, they managed to preserve their position and, indeed, benefit from it. Several kings visited the abbey, one of the last being Richard II in 1398.

The abbey received income from and held lands in other parts of Shropshire (such as at Atcham) and in Derbyshire and Leicestershire. Furthermore, at various times it benefited from exemptions to the tolls and taxes levied throughout the realm either by other landowners or by the Crown.

These privileges may have helped the abbey financially but did little to endear the canons to ordinary folk and tradesmen or to the increasing number of secular landowners. For many years the abbey was staffed by a large number of servants and was apparently more concerned with preserving the pleasures of secular, rather than the austere aspects of religious, life.

This was not always the case. At times the abbey tried to run its affairs with a laudable degree of self-sufficiency, often hindered by the unwanted task of tax and rent collection on behalf of the Crown and Papal impositions. Such work was not only time-consuming but also expensive to administer, particularly since the abbey's lands were dispersed over several counties. Furthermore, the abbey was expected to provide pensions, accommodation and other benefits to titled associates, visitors and the poor. Not all guests were a drain on the finances: Duke John of Gaunt rested at the abbey infirmary for two days in January 1398 after falling ill at the Shrewsbury Parliament. On leaving he presented the abbot with twenty pounds of gold to show his gratitude.

On several occasions abbots were instructed to reduce the number of servants enjoying free food and board and to desist from selling pensions where the subsequent drain on the abbey's finances was greater than the amount received from the person purchasing the pension. On one occasion in 1347, Abbot Henry granted a thresher named John of Garmston a corrody (free lodging) for as long as he lived. This charitable practice was quite common and undoubtedly strained the abbey's resources even further.

Some of the most stringent economies arose as a direct result of the Bubonic Plague (the 'Black Death') during the fourteenth century when the population was decimated by the spread of disease. Two abbots and several of the canons died between 1350 and 1353 and it is likely that up to a third of the local population perished as a direct result of the plague, ending up in

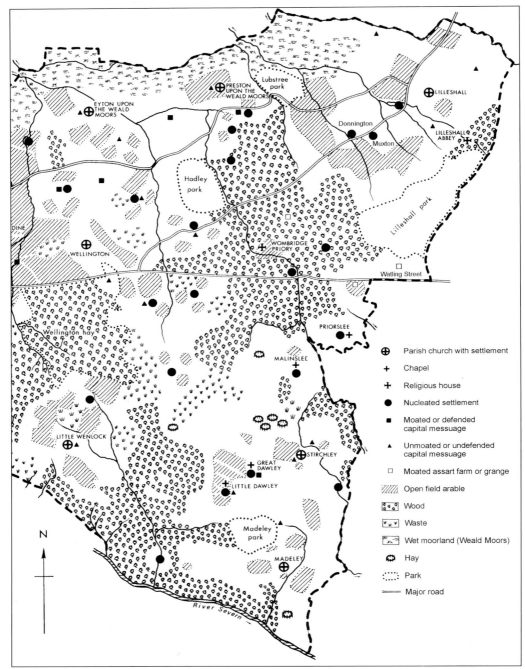

Extract from a fourteenth-century plan of the Telford area, reproduced with permission from the Victoria County History of Shropshire, *volume XI (1985). The plan shows the context of Donnington and Muxton in relation to the surrounding area. In fact, the woodland around Wombridge at this time extended further eastwards into the land depicted as arable open field to the south of Donnington.*

20

a lime-slaked communal burial pit. Many acres of cultivated land and animals had to be abandoned with consequent loss of both food supplies and income.

Fortunately, even though the plague dispersed and returned many times between then and the mid-seventeenth century, Donnington and its surrounding villages managed to avoid the total abandonment experienced elsewhere and so maintained a degree of continuity in occupation. Such was the impact of the Black Death that, for many years afterwards, events were recorded according to their proximity to this great pestilence. (A plague pit was discovered at Honnington in 1955 when the foundations for two bungalows were being dug out. It contained the skeletons of at least twenty-four people, including one child, and was dated to about 1650.)

In 1337 there were about 145 free tenants and their families in Lilleshall, Honnington, Donnington and Muxton, of which a third lived in Donnington. Recovery from the effects of the plague was very slow and even by 1563, almost two centuries later, the population had only attained a total of 84 households.

Financial difficulties continued throughout the remainder of the fourteenth and fifteenth centuries. Some abbots were too senile to understand how to combat the problem and were forbidden to make any decisions without prior consultation with their canons. Others tried to improve efficiency and reduce spending but were hindered by incompetence and self-interest. Although the abbey managed to maintain a fairly consistent reputation for spiritual rectitude together with academic and literary achievement, it was a sad fact that it was equally consistently inept at managing its financial affairs.

Whether the motivation for extending land ownership derived from a pressing need to meet its secular obligations or to improve the abbey's standard of living is a matter for debate; both probably featured at different times and were affected by general economic conditions.

There is no doubt, however, that the abbey's activities in increasing the size of its holdings led to an expansion of cultivated and occupied land in Muxton, Donnington and Donnington Wood. Successive abbots encouraged both arable farming and minor excursions into industrial activity (there must have been some iron-working and perhaps also coal digging at Quam Pool during the fourteenth century, when it was known as Qualmesmytthe – the smithy at Quam).

The population increased modestly and, because of the absence of any close-knit settlements in Donnington, the enclosure movement which affected much of lowland England in the fifteenth century, causing considerable social distress, had very little impact in this area.

However, the economic changes which occurred gradually throughout the Middle Ages caused a shift in the relative importance of the various social classes. Secular interests became stronger than spiritual as the part played by the middle class gained in importance. Furthermore, the abuses, scandals and ineptitude of religious orders throughout the kingdom caused considerable resentment to successive kings and commoners over a long period.

It could hardly have come as a surprise that such a powerful and unpredictable king as Henry VIII saw a wonderful opportunity to strike a blow against the Pope (which would please his nobility and the people) and at the same time benefit from an influx of money to his diminished treasury. He decided to become the head of the Church in England and suppress those institutions which had become so hated by the general population – the abbeys.

The income from all property owned by the abbey in 1535 had amounted to £324 0s 10d. Of this, £77 10s was derived from the Lilleshall estates, to which 'Donyngton' tenants and farms supplied £18 17s 2d. Although not a substantial amount it was respectable. However, it was by no means as much as it had been at its heyday during the early fourteenth century.

Lilleshall Abbey was dissolved on 16 October 1538 and on 28 November, together with the lands at Donnington, was leased to William Cavendish for one year. The abbot received a pension of £10 a year and a house in London and the remaining ten canons received pensions amounting to between £5 and £6 a year as well as gifts of between 40 and 50 shillings upon their departure. A total 'reward' of £28 15s 4d was divided between servants at the abbey upon its surrender to the Crown.

On 24 December 1539 Henry VIII sold entitlement to the abbey and its lands to a wealthy wool merchant, James Leveson (pronounced 'looson'), whose family had, in 1274, acquired the manor of Wolverhampton after having lived previously in Willenhall, Staffordshire. (Some accounts say that James acquired the abbey estates in 1544.) In addition to a one-off payment, James and his successors paid annual sums to the Crown.

Incidentally, Charles II decreed that the annual payments were to be given to the Pendrell family who had arranged for him to be hidden at Boscobel House following his flight from the Battle of Worcester in September 1651, in appreciation of their service to him at such a critical time.

The ownership of the Lilleshall lands by the Leveson family and their descendants during the ensuing 400 years was to have a far greater impact on the social and economic development of the area than anything that had gone before.

Detail from William Cartwright's Lilleshall estate map, 1679, showing the Old Lodge and nearby dwellings. The lodge balcony overlooked a plot of land known as Balcony Piece. Deer are shown to indicate that this is part of the Deer Park.

Four

The Leveson Influence

The Leveson family therefore became local magnates and proved to be able and just landlords, encouraging tenants to look after their properties, assisting them in the adoption of better farming methods, supporting them in times of strife and ensuring the legalities of Poor Law relief were observed. Industry, too, was encouraged.

The Leveson family were, at the time of acquiring the abbey estates, already reasonably wealthy and possessed estates in various parts of England. In common with other gentry (although on a much larger scale), they consciously sought to consolidate and expand their land holdings throughout the ensuing centuries, a fact which enabled them to manage their estates with a greater degree of efficiency. As well as most of Donnington and Lilleshall, the family owned considerable tracts in Priorslee and the areas now occupied by Stafford Park (named after the Lilleshall Company's Stafford Pit), Telford town centre and elsewhere in Shropshire, England, Wales and Scotland.

Their ancestry is well recorded elsewhere and is not within the scope of this book. Suffice it to say that, by a series of well considered marriages and alliances, the family's wealth and estates grew considerably over the years. They had a reputation for 'absorbing heiresses' and, rung by rung, climbed the social ladder until they became Dukes of Sutherland, the wealthiest family in Britain with enormous estates and business interests both at home and abroad.

Some Leveson descendants deserve a special mention because of their activities in this area.

Sir Richard Leveson appears to have lived for much of his life at the Old Lodge in Donnington Wood rather than in the abbey itself. When the disputes between Charles I and Parliament reached a head, Richard joined the king's side and, in October 1644, garrisoned the abbey with 160 untrained men conscripted from his Lilleshall estate, putting them under the governorship of Lord Bastwick, who died shortly afterwards. Command was then given to Major Duckinfield. Several skirmishes ensued with Parliamentary troops stationed at Longford Hall near Newport. Richard Baxter, the 'Puritan Divine' born at Rowton, was their chaplain. Baxter's father was taken captive and held at the abbey for a while.

In July 1645, Parliamentarians surrounded the abbey with trenches and earthworks to provide cover for musketeers. A siege began under the command of Major Braine. Contrary to popular belief, the abbey was not fired on from the top of Lilleshall Hill but rather from emplacements a regulatory distance from the abbey on the north side. The cannon fired relentlessly until the abbey buildings were in ruins and the walls breached. Major Duckinfield and many of the defenders perished and were buried in shallow graves. The garrison capitulated on 5 October 1645; survivors were allowed to depart leaving their weapons behind, including their hastily-made lead musket balls.

Eighteenth-century watercolour paintings of the Old Lodge.

The Civil War had a devastating effect on ordinary men and their families. They had little choice but to join their lord's army, irrespective of where their own sympathies lay. Richard Leveson enlisted from his own tenants and it may well be that whoever lived in a cottage on the main road at Donnington hid his savings in the ground, hoping to retrieve them when hostilities ended. He may have been killed during the siege at Lilleshall. Whatever the reason, he never returned to dig up his money and it was not until 1938 that the 'Donnington Treasure' was unearthed. (Details of that discovery are in Chapter Fourteen.)

Richard Leveson managed to retain his estates after the Civil War and remained at the Old Lodge in Donnington Wood until his death in 1661. Because Richard had no heir, the lands passed to Lady Katherine Gower (pronounced 'goor'), daughter of his deceased brother. Her son, Sir Thomas, was the first of the Leveson Gowers.

His successors also lived at the Old Lodge when residing in Shropshire until about 1776 after which they moved to the Old Hall in Lilleshall and, in 1831, to Lilleshall Hall. The latter two residences remained in their possession until the twentieth century.

Gamekeepers managed the Deer Park and the Old Lodge throughout the years even after hunting in the park ceased around 1700. Until then, gamekeepers were not only responsible for overseeing everyday life at the lodge but also for maintaining the shotguns and dogs, predominantly of the light or white coloured Talbot breed whose power of scent and heavy jaws were ideal for hunting. Spectators were able to view events from the balcony at the lodge.

At the time Cartwright's map of the estate was drawn for William Leveson Gower, William Whitmore was keeper at the lodge. He also leased a smallholding with cattle, pigs, geese and hens at The Hammers, so looking after the lodge may not have been a full time occupation. He died in September 1667. He was succeeded by Lewis Dale who died some two months later. Lewis's son James Dale took up the reins of office until his own death in 1706.

In 1720, tenants complained about the great nuisance caused by starving deer constantly breaking out of the park. By 1774, much of the park had been converted to fields although a few pockets of forest remained. The Old Lodge was demolished around 1820, possibly damaged by fire

Nineteenth-century sketch of the Old Lodge.

(a common hazard in timber framed buildings), or it may simply have become unsuitable for continued residence after years of neglect – expectations having changed with social standing.

Granville Leveson Gower was born in 1721. When his father John became Viscount Trentham (after the family's estates in Staffordshire) and 1st Earl Gower in 1746, Granville was given the courtesy title of Viscount Trentham and assumed the title 2nd Earl Gower when his father died in 1754. In 1786 he became 1st Marquis of Stafford. His decisions had a dramatic effect on the industrial and agricultural development of the Donnington area.

Granville had two sons. The eldest was George Granville Leveson Gower (2nd Earl Gower and 2nd Marquis of Stafford) who, in 1832 (a year before he died) was granted the title of 1st Duke of Sutherland (he had married the Countess of Sutherland in 1785, hence the connection). The second son, also named Granville, was created 1st Earl Granville in 1833. To confuse matters further, Earl Granville's oldest male descendants also had, and continue to have, Granville as one of their forenames.

Successive Earls Gower and Granville were to continue the policies inaugurated by the 1st Earl Gower. The fact that many streets and industrial works – even the Granville Country Park – are named after them reflects the long period of occupation, power and influence they had in the area.

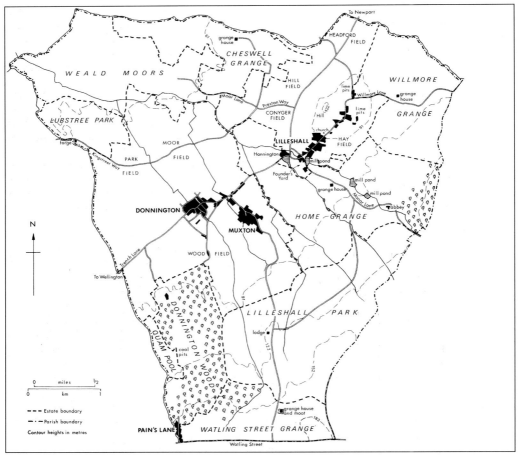

The extent of seventeenth-century Lilleshall Parish, reproduced with permission from the Victoria County History of Shropshire, *volume XI (1985).*

26

Five

Farming

It is highly probable that the earliest farming activity in the Donnington area took place well before the Romans erected their original small fort at Uxacona on Red Hill around AD 50. Coins dating from Emperor Vespasian's time (69-79) and other small items like brooches have been found nearby, indicating a long period of occupation. The fort remnants lie by and beneath a reservoir alongside Watling Street. Soldiers required fresh food and refreshment, so it is not unreasonable to assume that nearby farm enclosures, however small, met that need. We do know that a small Iron Age enclosure existed on the site of Castle Farm at Priorslee; it is now submerged beneath a lake at junction 4 of the M54.

Another reasonable assumption is that the area continued to be inhabited and that Saxons were next to make their mark here. We can be fairly certain that one of their earliest settlements was in the vicinity of Donnington Farm (currently the White House Hotel). It made sense to live near an established trackway (possibly between settlements at Wellington and Lilleshall) simply because it afforded an easier line of communication with them.

If this was so, it is also reasonable to assume that a similar farmstead existed near the even more important trade route, Watling Street. Perhaps a Saxon farm was on the ruins of Uxacona itself. Or even at Watling Street Grange. And it would have been quite feasible for the two farmsteads to be joined by another trackway leading from north to south. We may never know.

From the time of the Norman Conquest at least, Donnington, Muxton and Donnington Wood were traditional farming areas characterised by scattered farmsteads with equally scattered fields carved out of the forest over the centuries. Ownership boundaries within and on the edge of the forest often took the form of long trenches; one created in the thirteenth century gave its name to Trench, the township adjoining Donnington to the west.

Very few farmers owned the property they occupied and tended; they were usually tenants of lords and other individuals who held parcels of land in the vicinity. Apart from minor changes in ownership there was little in the way of development. In fact, in times of plague or war it was virtually impossible to find either buyers or new tenants for farms whose occupants had perished or fled. Consequently it was not unusual for fields to revert to scrubland or grass for considerable periods until circumstances improved. Because farmers paid part of their rent in the form of produce, landlords were also affected by adverse economic climates.

The number of farm labourers employed by these tenant farmers greatly depended on how much land they tended and whether they could afford to support others besides their own family. Serfdom was, of course, commonplace but serfs required feeding and accommodating. Those which did exist lived in the farmer's household.

Farming was supported by ancillary trades and craftsmen such as wheelwrights and carpenters for making carts, coopers for making casks for storing liquids and butter as well as blacksmiths who not only shod horses but also made a variety of implements. The Humbers, long associated with Donnington, was a small settlement where smithies were located. The Humbers is a corruption of 'The Hammers', the name by which it was known in 1685.

To help combat the effects of the plague, it became common practice to turn out increased numbers of sheep and pigs on land which had, because of the lack of farmers, reverted to pasture. The majority of farming at this time would have been at Donnington on either side of the old Wellington-Newport road and along Muxton Lane; very little would have been permitted in Donnington Wood because of its forest status.

During the Middle Ages, tenants lived on a virtually meat-free diet of sheep's milk and cheese, rye bread, various grain products, peas and beans plus whatever else they were able to grow in the small gardens attached to their dwellings. Creatures, such as hares, rabbits and wildfowl, were often taken from the forest (but not wild boar or the lord's deer).

Sheep were seldom reared for their meat and it was quite rare for a tenant farmer to keep more than a couple of cows for their milk unless he was contracted to supply the abbey. Those animals he ate were likely to be sick or dying. Goats, once commonplace, caused so much damage to the neighbourhood that numbers were kept in check to minimise problems with the landowner and other farmers. Pig husbandry was widespread. Separate pastureland for rearing animals was unusual; they tended to wander through the woodland in search of food. This was an ancient right with certain access limitations imposed at the landowner's discretion.

Above: *Donnington Farm, c. 1910. By 1940 the building had become the White House Hotel.*
Opposite: *Particulars of Donnington Farm as detailed in the Lilleshall Estate sale catalogue, 1914.*

LOT 88.

(Coloured Yellow on Plan No. 2.)

An Exceedingly well situated and Compact

CORN GROWING & FEEDING FARM,

KNOWN AS

"DONNINGTON FARM,"

COMPRISING

Excellent House and Grounds, very extensive Buildings, 6 Cottages and Gardens,

AND

367 Acres of Arable, Pasture and Meadow Land.

*Tenant :—*REPRESENTATIVES OF THE LATE MR. EDWARD JAMES.

THE HOMESTEAD is exceptionally well situated and is easily accessible from the main Road, and from all parts of the Farm. It is directly adjacent to Donnington Station.

THE HOUSE stands back at a short distance from the main road and is quite secluded therefrom ; it contains—

On the Ground Floor—Lounge Hall, Drawing Room (23 ft. 6 ins. × 16 ft. 9 ins.) with large **Bay Window** ; Dining Room (15 ft. 9 in. × 15 ft. 6 in.) with Bay Window ; Morning Room (15 ft. × 14 ft.) with Bay Window ; Well lighted large Kitchen, Pantry, Butler's Pantry, **Back Kitchen**, Scullery, Laundry, Dairy and Store Rooms.

In the Basement are 2 Cellars and 2 Wine Bins.

On the First Floor—Six Bedrooms, Bath Room, w.c., and Housemaid's Pantry, Man's Room.

On the Second Floor—6 Bed and Store Rooms.

Gas and Water are laid on and there is also a good supply of Water from Pump.

THE GROUNDS are tastefully and nicely laid out and comprise Pleasure and Kitchen Gardens, **Lawn** and Shrubberies, Tennis Lawn and Orchard. There is a Tool House and Potting Shed in **Garden.**

THE BUILDINGS are very extensive and conveniently arranged and possess accommodation as follows : Trap House, Hackney Stable and Loose Box, Harness Room, Motor Garage, Petrol Store, Stabling for 10 Cart Horses, 2 large Loose Boxes, 4 Cow Sheds with tying for 57, served by tramways ; 4 Open Yards with Feeding and Shelter Sheds, Sheds to accommodate 48 Cattle.

Pig Yard and 3 Sties, Loose Box, 2 Poultry Houses, Sheep Bath and Shed, 4-bay Implement Shed, Implement Shed, 8-bay Cart Shed, Carpenter's and Blacksmith's Shops.

Water is laid on to several Tanks about the Buildings.

THE ADMINISTRATIVE PORTION comprises Turbine House (with Turbine which is driven by Water from a Reservoir supplied by Brook No. 638, and controlled by a Weir and Sluice ; this forms an excellent Motive power for all Machinery) ; Root House, Mixing House, Meal House, Cutting Loft, extensive Fodder Lofts, Cake and Corn Granary, Corn Barn, Boiling House, Meal and Potato Store.

2 Nine-Bay Dutch Barns (each 135 ft. by 24 ft.)

In Field No. 519 there is a Shippon.

SIX CAPITAL COTTAGES WITH GARDENS

Nos. 42, 44, 31, 33, 35 Donnington and 15 Humber Lane.

*Sub-Tenants :—*MESSRS. WINNALL, LOWE, HARRIS, WATKIN, WORRALL, and MORRIS.

THE LAND is well served by good Roads ; the soil is a light loam which is very friable, highly productive and eminently suitable for the growth of root and grain crops. The Pastures show a good herbage and are well watered. The whole has been well farmed for many years. Fields Nos. 705, 704 & 706, are exceedingly well situated, having frontage to the main Road and being directly adjacent to the Midland Iron Works and to Donnington Station ; they are therefore admirably suitable as Building Sites.

The Sporting Rights form a very considerable asset.

Throughout the Middle Ages, sheep rearing was the mainstay of the English economy and virtually every farmer was expected to do his best to keep up production for the wool trade. Indeed, wool was such an important product that it was law for everyone to be buried in a woollen shroud! It is because of the fortune made by trading in wool that the Leveson family were able to purchase the abbey estate from King Henry VIII.

Cultivated crops were labour intensive until the twentieth century. The land had to be ploughed using oxen borrowed from the landlord and other tenant farmers. (Horses suitable for this work were not in general use until the sixteenth century). Crops had to be weeded (although this was seldom done with any enthusiasm or regularity), harvested, allowed to dry, gathered and stored. Apart from the plough and sickle, and horse (or mule or donkey) and cart, there were few aids available; almost everything relied on back-breaking manual labour, whatever the weather.

Hemp (to make linen) and flax (for ropes, later used in local mines) were commonly grown. Cattle were replacing sheep by 1540 because the wool trade had declined. The economic and social condition of England gradually changed throughout the late seventeenth and early eighteenth centuries. Landowners were forced to consider seriously the financial position of their estates and find means to increase production if they and their tenants were to survive. This was the period referred to as the 'Agrarian Revolution' during which new and improved methods of farming were introduced and prosperity among the larger landowners and middle classes increased. The growing of potatoes and varieties of root crops such as turnips and carrots helped to vary an otherwise uninspiring diet.

Strip farming, the normal but inefficient method of dividing cultivated land between villagers throughout the Middle Ages, was replaced (at the request of the tenants and with the agreement of Sir William Leveson) by land consolidations where farmers benefited from enlarged, undivided fields for their sole, no longer shared, use. It is probable that some land in the deer park was released for agricultural use at this time. However, the availability of common land was reduced and restrictions ('stints') were placed on the number of animals a farmer might be permitted to graze on certain tracts. Pig farming was greatly affected by increased encroachment into the forest (pigs had previously been permitted to forage in the

Donnington Wood Farm, c. 1910. It is from this farm that Farm Lane is named.

30

Donnington Wood.

LOT 18.

(Coloured Grey on Plan No. 1.)

A well situated and amply equipped

FEEDING and CORN GROWING FARM

KNOWN AS

" DONNINGTON WOOD FARM "

COMPRISING

Good House, Extensive Buildings, 4 Cottages, and 270 Acres of First Class Arable and Pasture Land.

Tenant :—Mr. T. H. Ward.

THE HOMESTEAD is situate within a short distance of Donnington Station, in the heart of a densely populated District ; and Roads emanate therefrom to all parts of the Farm.

THE HOUSE is pleasantly situated and contains :—Drawing, Dining and Morning Rooms, Good Kitchen, Dairy, Pantry and 5 Bedrooms, approached by Front and Back Staircases ; Back Kitchen and Store Room off Courtyard.

There is a good Garden, well stocked with Fruit Trees, and a Lawn.

THE BUILDINGS are conveniently arranged and possess the following accommodation :—Five Cowsheds with tying for 49, served by Feeding Passages, Four Loose Boxes to accommodate 16 Cattle, Three Open Yards with Feeding Sheds for 40 Cattle, Stabling for 12 Cart Horses, good Loose Box, Lambing Yard with Shelter Shed and two Loose Boxes, 4 Pig Styes, two-stall Hackney Stable, Saddle Room, Boiling House, Wain House, Sheep Bath and Shelter, 4-bay Cart Shed, Poultry Yard with Sitting Boxes.

THE ADMINISTRATIVE PORTION comprises :—Engine House, Root House, Mixing House, Straw Bay, Cutting Loft, very extensive Fodder Lofts, large Corn Granaries, Cake, Corn and Meat Granaries, large Store House, Boiling and Meal Houses.

THREE 4-BAY DUTCH BARNS

Each 60 feet by 24 feet.

FOUR GOOD COTTAGES WITH GARDENS

Nos. 8 and 11, Wellington Road, and Nos. 3 and 5 Farm Lane.

Sub-Tenants :—Messrs. Coppick, Beech, Doody & Palin.

THE LAND comprises 145 Acres of exceedingly Fertile and Friable Arable and 124 Acres of Productive and well Watered Pastures, the whole is in a very high state of Cultivation.

The Sporting Rights form a very considerable Asset.

TIMBER :—Included with the Freehold of this Lot is the Growing Timber thereon, estimated to have a value of £36 2s. 0d.

Particulars of Donnington Wood Farm as detailed in the Lilleshall Estate sale catalogue, 1914.

undergrowth at certain times of the year). With less woodland available, rearing pigs became more of a domestic activity with the animals kept in a sty in the back yard or at the bottom of the garden. They were fed on a mixture of barley, dried peas and stale beer. This practice continued well into the mid-twentieth century. Women were allowed to cook but never kill or cure (cut up and salt) pigs in case they tainted the meat; this was the sole province of men.

Elsewhere in Shropshire these changes caused considerable social upheaval; enclosure of common land and small farms together with the eviction of agricultural labourers were frequent, leaving many folk destitute and forcing them to migrate to other areas. During the same period the East Shropshire Coalfield (reaching from the Severn Gorge to Donnington Wood) was embarking on an entirely different type of revolution – industrial.

Earl Gower was a major force in the development of efficient farming methods and industry. A man of astute business acumen and holder of various high political offices, he effected many major alterations on his estates: mainly by agreement but, when necessary, by Act of Parliament. He enclosed large parts of Donnington and neighbouring Lilleshall and introduced a series of reforms which led to the enlargement, reshaping and draining of land to render it more productive.

For much of the seventeenth century the East Shropshire Coalfield was the second largest coal-producing area in Britain, after Durham/Northumbria. Coal, and the availability of substantial siderite (iron ore) deposits, led to the birth of an iron industry of unprecedented proportions. Labour was required for the mines and furnaces and, because of the dangerous nature of the work, wages were high. Many of those dispossessed of their rural livelihoods drifted into the area in search of work. As their numbers increased so did the pressures on the agricultural community to produce more and more food. Earl Gower's improvements, particularly in land drainage and new buildings for farming purposes, enabled this to be achieved. It was at this time that greater emphasis was placed on dairy produce. It was also at this time that rents for tenant farmers were hiked up considerably; they doubled between 1750 and 1805. By far their greatest outgoing was rent.

Between 1810 and 1820 major improvements were made: new farm buildings were erected and fields enlarged and rationalised; farmers were expected to adopt new methods of food production and land maintenance. Drainage and access roads were improved. Before long the areas to the north and south of Donnington Wood were characterised by vast acres of reasonably level fields and isolated but well-constructed farmhouses, with occasional tracts of woodland to reduce the risk of soil erosion. Tenants were employed to quarry cinders and slag from the Donnington ironworks to improve roads (which were, in reality, little more than lanes) in the district – the tenants were then charged with the expense as the work was done for their benefit! However, other features began to appear much larger than before between the fields and trees; increased mining activity gave rise to bigger spoil heaps. The dirt and heavy clay extracted had to go somewhere.

Bearing in mind that the majority of the first wage-earning miners had previously worked as farm labourers, it comes as no surprise that they provided much needed help to local farmers, especially at harvest time. They were experienced and hard working. It reminded them of what it was like to work with nature, in the open air and not inside the dark and dangerous depths in search of coal and ironstone. The practice of some miners helping with the harvest continued until the closure of the Granville Colliery in 1979. A little extra is always useful.

The period between 1875 and the outbreak of the First World War was possibly the worst to be experienced by British farmers since the plague years of the fourteenth century. Frequent adverse weather conditions led to a succession of failed harvests. Problems were compounded by increased imports of cheap food, especially grain, from North America, Australia and New Zealand. The 'Great Depression' in British farming had a devastating impact everywhere.

The drastic effects of this decline were stemmed to some degree by the Duke of Sutherland (along with other large estate owners) reducing farm rents (by up to 20%) and providing funds for further land improvements. However, it became obvious that the situation was unlikely to improve. In 1912 the first of the Lilleshall Estate auctions took place to release the Sutherland family from some of their capital-draining responsibilities. Over 8,600 acres of land and a large number of farmhouses and cottages were sold.

Existing tenants in Donnington, Donnington Wood and Muxton jumped at the chance to purchase their homes at bargain prices, hoping to make good profits during the wartime boom in productivity and prices. Further land and property was auctioned off in 1914 and 1917. Edward James purchased Donnington Farm and several nearby cottages as dwellings for his farm workers; T.H. Ward acquired several farms, including Donnington Wood Farm and Lubstree Park; in 1979 the Ward family also farmed The Hincks and Watling Street Grange. The Leveson Gower influence on local life embarked on a gradual but inevitable decline.

Between 1870 and 1918, almost a third of farm labourers left the land and sought alternative employment because it was no longer possible to employ cheap juvenile labour following the introduction of compulsory elementary education for minors. In contrast, the wages of those labourers who remained rose from an average of 12s 3d to £1 17s for a fifty-hour week.

Farming suffered a general decline during the inter-war years although impressive new machinery was introduced, particularly the tractor which, with an increasing number of attachments, was able to perform a variety of functions hitherto done painstakingly (and slowly) by man and horse. Farmers began to band together to share the cost of machinery and increased their bargaining power with buyers and food processing companies. The number of labourers employed on the land reduced further. Even farmers' sons were encouraged to seek better employment outside the industry.

Greater efficiencies were made possible by further field enlargement, although the transfer of Woolwich Arsenal shortly before the outbreak of the Second World War caused a considerable reduction in land used for agricultural purposes both north and south of the old Wellington-Newport road. Smaller pocket-sized fields around Donnington Wood, surrounded as they were by spoil heaps and wasteland, afforded less opportunity for development. All was not doom and gloom, however. The sugar beet factory at Allscott, near Wellington, opened in 1927. Farmers were quick to take the government subsidies intended to encourage beet cultivation. Similarly, milk production increased dramatically after 1933 when the Milk Marketing Board guaranteed minimum prices.

The Second World War brought increased production in essential produce, such as beef, milk, eggs, cereals, potatoes and sugar and, unlike the brief prosperity during the First World War, subsidies continued afterwards. Women formed a sizeable proportion of 'the land army', assuming the labouring role previously undertaken by men. Partly because of increased use of farm machinery, fertilisers and herbicides, the number of farm labourers suffered a further decline of some 40% between 1949 and 1965, although the Agricultural Workers Union was able to negotiate better pay and working conditions (including shorter hours), particularly during the 1970s and 1980s. Nevertheless, farm work remained one of the most poorly paid types of skilled work. Wrekin Farmers began in 1977 and provides additional co-operative farming facilities and assistance to the few farms, albeit with larger acreage, still in existence.

Farming (including the twentieth-century phenomenon of 'pick your own' produce) is mainly confined to the north of the Wellington-Newport road, the south along Watling Street and east of Muxton. The Central Ordnance Depot is itself responsible for the closure of farms and the dramatic loss of much farmland. Apart from some isolated fields and land preserved (for the time being at least) for recreational purposes (including the Granville Country Park and The Bell Field), much of the area is given over to domestic housing, retail outlets, business premises and even a waste disposal site. It comes as no surprise that many

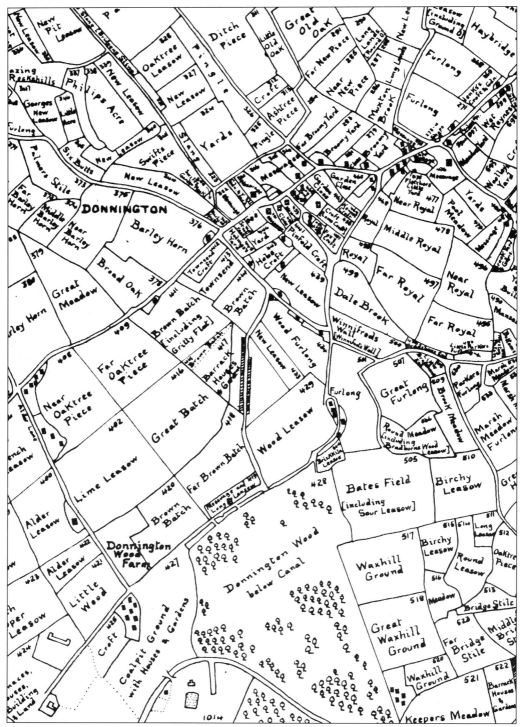

Extract from an 1813 tithe map of Lilleshall Parish, showing field names and the locations of 'messuages' (dwellings) and the Donnington Barracks along what is now School Road.

34

people these days are ignorant of what farming entails. The public's demand for cheap food together with the buying power of modern supermarkets means that farming, instead of being an important facet of the country's economy, has become sidelined and uneconomic; without government subsidy, many farms would close.

There is still some evidence of former agricultural activity. Historically, virtually every field in the country was given a name and Donnington was no exception. This practice was essential for several reasons. Landowners needed to identify which precise plots of ground were subject to a tenancy agreement. Farmers needed to direct their labourers to specific fields in order to carry out sowing and harvesting. Children and wives needed to know to which field they should take their labouring husbands' bread, cheese and water or beer lunches. New fields were created by continued incursions into forest and waste land as well as by dividing existing fields into smaller units.

Most of the field names are purely descriptive. 'Gore' refers to a triangular piece of ground, whereas 'Gorsty' means land upon which gorse grew. 'Leasows' (from the Old English 'leaswe') is land used for pastoral farming. It was normal practice to combine descriptive elements, as in Wood Leasow, the 'meadow next to the wood' A field on a rise might be called Meadow Bank. 'Royals' were fields in which rye (for making bread) was grown.

Trees often feature in field names, as in Yewtree, Birchy and Alder Leasows. Rookery (where rooks' nests proliferated) and Rough or Stony Ground were also descriptive. Water features are also common, as in Lower and Upper Pool Field and Brook Yard. Waxhill is suggestive of a field where bees were nurtured (perhaps in conjunction with the grounds of the Old Lodge), although it may refer to the location of a small Saxon farmstead.

Some names relate to activity by man; Coalpit Ground, Donnington Wood above Canal, Keeper's Leasow (near the Old Lodge) and Barn Field are typical examples. Perhaps one of the most puzzling field names is 'Bradshaws and Roaring Meg' in the south near St Georges, owned or created by someone called Bradshaw at a time when a cannon nicknamed Roaring Meg made a name for itself in the siege of Londonderry in 1689.

Field names were an important feature of farming life. It is a pity that modern names, of streets for example, do not always preserve their previous existence for posterity, nor reflect the use to which particular parcels of ground were put.

Key figures in early industrial development. Top left: William Reynolds; bottom left: Thomas Gilbert; right: Granville Leveson Gower (2nd Earl Gower, later 1st Marquis of Stafford).

The Donnington Wood Canal looking westwards, c. 1930. By this time the canal was no longer in commercial use although locals still used it for fishing.

Six

Activities to 1800

Man's nature has always been to explore alternative and additional ways of providing extra income for himself and his family. Apart from trades associated with farming, the economic and social conditions at any given time dictate the degree of industrial progress, if any, that can be achieved.

Before the Norman Conquest, wood was the main source of fuel and most implements. Iron tools and weapons would have been made in small, probably temporary, furnaces built only when there was a need or when sufficient quantities of ironstone had been collected over a period. The amount of ironworking carried on in this area before, during and after Roman occupation was, at most, limited. Coal was certainly used at the city of Viroconium near Atcham at some time during its lifetime and was probably extracted from elsewhere in the East Shropshire Coalfield. The same applies to ironworking. The Romans would have discovered outcrops of fungous coal at The Nabb near Oakengates while laying Watling Street.

After the Norman Conquest, few opportunities for 'industrial' development actually arose for many years, partly because of the rigid structure of society and the devastating effects of successive plagues and epidemics. Civil war gave an occasional impetus for weapon and armour development but did not do much for long-term prospects. People were more concerned with survival than development.

The coal seams at the Freehold and Muxtonbridge mines dip sharply and are severely faulted. Others in Donnington Wood, near the modern townships of St Georges and Wrockwardine Wood, were so close to the surface that coal and ironstone could be extracted by digging shallow pits, often no more than 25m deep. It was this ease of extraction which gave rise to coal digging on a small scale during the Middle Ages. (Indeed, the practice was revived for a short while during the General Strike of 1926 when locals, desperate to obtain supplies when the mines were closed, dug their own illegal pits near St Georges.) Ironstone extraction was a by-product of coal mining and a smithy at Quam Pool is the first one documented in the area, in 1277. The iron was probably picked out by hand from pit waste (a commonplace practice from the eighteenth century onwards). Coal was being dug by 1330 when its total annual value was one pound.

In the fifteenth century there was a lane called Coalpyt Way. By 1580 there were water-driven hammer forges at The Humbers pool (where a mill had previously stood), but the first substantial iron furnace, the precise location of which is not known, seems to have been introduced by Richard and Vincent Corbett in 1591, when Sir Richard Leveson granted them a lease. It was fired by charcoal. The first recorded coal mine (as opposed to shallow pit) in Donnington Wood was operating by 1592.

The Levesons continued to lease short-term, small-scale mining rights to successive tenants. In 1674, Francis Charlton of Apley Castle near Wellington took a twenty-one-year lease after which surface coal deposits at Donnington Wood were all but exhausted. Nevertheless, profits were minimal. Only surface coal had been exploited because of the expense involved in digging deeper. In fact, the prospects of success were so limited economically that no further leases were granted between 1695 and 1715.

However, events were taking place elsewhere which would soon change the economics of exploitation. The Industrial Revolution was taking root in Coalbrookdale and south of the River Severn. By 1750, activities had advanced to Old Park, Horsehay and Ketley. The problems associated with the potentially high cost of mineral exploitation in Donnington Wood suddenly seemed irrelevant. Demand was increasing at such a pace that deeper mining operations in the vicinity of the Old Lodge would soon be an economic proposition.

There were still other problems to be overcome. No established roads linked Donnington Wood with Ketley or Horsehay, where the demand for coal and iron were greatest. Furthermore, there would be a problem with drainage in any mines dug in the area as the water table was relatively high. Granville Leveson Gower (2nd Earl Gower) leased mining rights to James Barber in 1756. The Earl, like many landed gentry at that time, was keen to develop the mineral resources for his own gain and terminated Barber's lease in order to form a mining partnership, Earl Gower & Company, in 1764. In any event, the Earl was concerned with Barber's apparent inability to work the mines properly. Nevertheless, many pits continued to be operated by chartermasters in the same year; among them were William Barker, John Beard, Arthur, Thomas and William Cooper, Joseph Clayton, Richard Lowe, Robert Mannering, Allen Pickering, Thomas Pitchford, John Price, George Simon and William Wakefield. They did not confine themselves to sinking pits; Thomas Davies, for example, made bricks.

The Earl Gower partnership concentrated its efforts on the limestone and coal trades rather than iron because they considered the competition in the latter field too great. However, Abraham Darby II (in 1756) and subsequently his son-in-law Richard Reynolds (in 1764) leased iron mines from Earl Gower & Company and transported ore to their new blast furnaces at Horsehay.

Many of the East Shropshire Coalfield partnerships at that time were combinations of landed interests and technical skills, and several partnerships altered their constitution as partners died and others replaced them. The landed gentry employed agents to act for them in the running of their estates; successful agents could be expected to prove valuable business partners. One such was John Gilbert who became a partner with his brother Thomas in Earl Gower & Company. Gilbert had been agent for the Duke of Bridgwater who made his mark on the country's economy by the construction of the first commercially viable canal in Britain.

Earl Gower's second wife Louisa was the Duke's sister, and it was through this connection that Gilbert arrived in Shropshire with a view to assisting the Earl in his business ventures. Work began almost immediately on the construction of the first canal in Shropshire running from the Earl's limestone quarries at Lilleshall to the coal mines at Donnington Wood. Tenant farmers affected by the proposed route (George Wheeler, William Walding, John Hall, Robert Dawes, Richard Mansell among others) received compensation for the inconvenience and loss of farmland.

The full 5½ mile length was open by 1768. Traffic was two-way. A wharf was built at Pave Lane near Newport, where coal was taken for sale elsewhere in the West Midlands. Some coal was used in the lime-kilns at Lilleshall and lime brought to Donnington Wood for use in the local furnaces. Lime unsuitable for the furnaces was used to improve the soil on the Gower-rented farms in the area. Important points were that the canal now made transport of materials much easier and the drainage difficulties in the mines was solved, providing that steam engines (such as the one at Muxtonbridge, where much of the building still remains) continued to pump flood water from the pits to keep the canal fully stocked. There were no locks on the canal. Offshoots to the canal ran underground to connect with navigable levels inside the pits at Donnington Wood. By the end of the century there were several branches into various parts of Lilleshall and at the western end links were made with the rest of the East Shropshire Coalfield, even to the River Severn at Coalport, by a series of ingenious inclines and locks. The canal was initially called 'Earl Gower's Canal', then 'Marquis of Stafford's Tub-Boat Canal' (in 1786, when the company also changed its name) then 'The Duke of Sutherland's Canal' (in 1832 when the second Marquis assumed that title) and, finally, simply 'The Donnington Wood Canal'.

The efficiency and economic viability of the canal system was second to no other transport system at that time and it was for this reason that many of the great iron-making partnerships co-operated with one another to finance and plan the coalfield network.

In 1788 William Reynolds and Joseph Rathbone leased land from Earl Gower for the building of blast furnaces at Donnington Wood, smelting ore from Wrockwardine Wood. The Earl himself invested £2,000 in the enterprise, an event common at a time when new partnerships were being created and profits could be high. John Bishton acquired the Donnington Wood furnaces in 1792 and later put them under Lilleshall Company control.

Before the existence of the canal network, minerals were transported in horse-drawn carts on wooden tramways, later replaced with cast iron rails. In 1788 a railway was laid between Donnington Wood and Ketley with a link to the Horsehay foundries. The wagons, made of wood and with iron wheels, were capable of carrying $2\frac{1}{2}$ tons of ore each and required three horses to haul them.

Various types of canal vessels were used in the area, the most common being those designed specifically for use at Donnington Wood. These were 3-ton square-ended tub boats, each 20 feet long and 6 feet 4 inches wide, costing about £20 each but with an unlimited life-span. One horse could be harnessed to pull up to 20 laden boats tied together in a long row. Although slow, the system was reliable, efficient and cost effective. Roads and tramways were used only where there was no canal.

The Lilleshall Estate, rich as it was in mineral wealth, developed rapidly as an industrial centre. Much building took place, including pithead and mine buildings, furnaces, wharves, offices and barrack houses to accommodate the growing workforce, many of whom migrated from the mines around Madeley. Barrack houses were situated close to where their occupants, including women and children, worked and, because they were surrounded by trees and industrial workings (but not too close to villages or farms), the area resembled a hastily-constructed frontier settlement.

Early mine workings had one combined entrance and exit, a highly dangerous situation should the roof collapse. Coal-laden baskets carried on backs had been replaced to some extent as early as the fourteenth century by barrows and sledges. By the end of the sixteenth century, wooden rails carried wooden wagons pushed or pulled by the workers. It is probable that a combination of these methods continued well into the eighteenth century, much depending on the size of the mine and its estimated worth. By the late eighteenth century, the wooden rails were covered with iron strips and the use of horses for underground haulage became more commonplace.

The area surrounding Donnington Wood already displayed the unmistakable signs of exploitation. Barren grey clay spoil tips rose close to the mine workings, covering all trace of previous habitation and earlier industrial activity. Adits and 'bell' pit shafts were abandoned, their holes left unfilled and unprotected. Footpaths between mines became overgrown when new ones were created for the latest shafts. Pithead gear, in the form of horse gins with flax ropes, decayed and fell apart. It is impossible to determine how many pits were sunk, worked and left to flood or be covered by spoil heaps between 1600 and 1800, but the scars they left behind would be nothing compared to what would follow. A map of 1788 shows over 100 mines in Donnington Wood, some connected to the underground canal system.

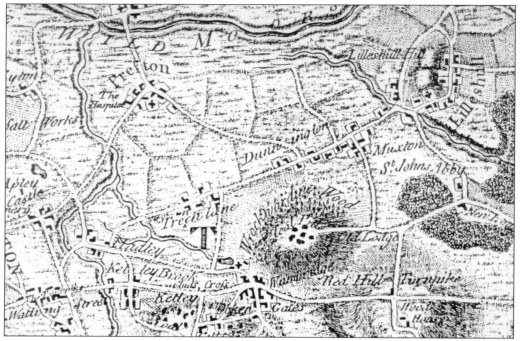

Detail from John Rocque's map of Shropshire, 1752. Donnington Wood is not shown but covers the eastern part of the area designated as Wrockwardine Wood.

Detail from Robert Baugh's map of Shropshire, 1808.

Earl Gower undoubtedly appreciated the value of his estates' resources and with his partners sought other ways of increasing income. Activities were expanded by ploughing profits back into the business. More efficient plant and machinery were acquired in an effort to increase production even further; for example, in 1779 the Gilbert brothers purchased a Boulton & Watt steam engine for pumping water out of the mines, making it possible to sink deeper shafts. Subsequently Earl Gower & Company purchased at least eighteen winding-engines for pitheads, together with several boilers.

These were essential if mining operations were to continue. Richer, deeper seams of coal in the eastern part of the area required high investment to enable longer galleries to be dug out and accessibility maintained. Eventually the galleries ran for several miles (as far as Lilleshall), getting deeper and deeper to extract more coal from the dipping seams. Contrary to popular belief, mining for coal was not the main reason why there were so many high flat-topped pit mounds dominating the Donnington Wood landscape; it was because of the frantic search for nodules of iron ore which could only be obtained by extracting vast quantities of clay from the depths. The clay was levelled and washed down with water to expose the ore which was then picked out by hand, usually by women and children.

Iron ore was much more profitable than coal; mining rights in Donnington Wood were highly prized and sought after by many of the furnace owners in the area who were largely responsible for the expansion of the Chartermaster system of mine management. Earl Gower's income rose by continued investment in ventures and leasing rights; miners benefited from fairly regular work. Those in between hoped to make excellent profits.

The foundations had been laid for industrial consolidation, exploitation and expansion on a scale hitherto unseen.

But what of the ordinary people? Mention has already been made of the revival of the enclosure movement throughout England and its effects on the rural population. The eighteenth century witnessed a mass exodus of folk from the countryside to the new centres of industry. Many of those who settled in the Donnington Wood area came from south Shropshire and Montgomeryshire; it was exceptional for migrants to travel any great distance in search of work, although a few men who had specialist occupations (such as stonemasons) arrived from the Cheshire-Staffordshire border into the area; their experience could be put to good use. A few became chartermasters.

As the industrial population increased it became necessary to erect more dwellings. Initially workers settled in small, scattered cottages, hurriedly built near the mine shafts, furnaces and kilns where they toiled. Before long this proved to be insufficient, and the Gower Company rectified the situation to some extent by constructing long rows of Barrack Houses, the major ones being at Waxhill (alongside the canal) and Donnington Wood, along what is now School Road. (Barrack houses at Queens Road do not appear on the 1813 tithe map of Lilleshall Parish, so were presumably erected shortly after that date.)

In those days the area was little more than a bleak frontier settlement, surrounded by pit mounds and spoil heaps. Most of the barracks were single-storey terraced dwellings, usually comprising a dirt-floor living room with a small coal fireplace, one bedroom and storehouse, and a communal wash-house with water standpipe and earth closet to be shared by each row. Some time later, a small pig sty was erected at the bottom of most gardens where vegetables were grown to supplement the diet and save money. The practice began of taking it in turns for each household to brew its own beer or share out portions of its pig, snared rabbits and woodfowl. People had very few possessions, virtually no furniture and seldom a change of clothes.

Residents of Donnington and Muxton fared a little better, partly because they didn't work in the mines but mainly because they were farm workers, plied a particular trade or, exceptionally, had private income. The same may be said of the few folk who lived in small

Donnington Barracks along what is now School Road, c. 1930. The photograph was taken by Reg Morgan from his shop beside the 'shut', or opening between two rows of houses. They were called 'barracks' because they resembled communal accommodation provided for soldiers at military establishments. Notice the barrels used to collect rainwater; none of the houses were provided with an internal water supply. These particular houses were demolished during the early 1950s.

cottages near The Bell field, some of which appear to have been erected towards the later years of the eighteenth century.

Until 1820, Donnington Wood workers' dwellings were usually leased by middlemen who had no qualms about exploiting the occupants, with little or no attention paid to sanitation, overcrowding or maintenance. Nevertheless, living conditions were considerably better than in rural areas and large cities. This, and the prospect of comparatively high wages, gave added momentum to the movement of population into Donnington Wood.

However, house occupation was tied to maintaining a job at one of the pits; quitting or being fired from the job inevitably meant being evicted and having to find somewhere else to work and live; only those absolutely desperate would throw themselves at the mercy of the Union Workhouses at Wellington or Shifnal. The threat of unemployment gave employers a very strong hand when it came to deciding who was to be employed and even the number of hours to be worked. Shortened hours, and hence reduced pay, could be almost as devastating as unemployment.

The close proximity of farmland to the new settlements precluded any difficulties in feeding the industrial workforce. For many years, even well into the nineteenth century, summertime presented problems to the mine owners because labourers left in large numbers to work in the fields, returning to the mines after harvests had been gathered. This was not so much because it was more pleasant to work in the open air, but rather because traditions were strong among a predominantly farm-reared population. The practice survived, in a part-time capacity, until well into the 1970s in both Donnington and neighbouring Priorslee.

Life was extremely hard at that time. Relatively high wages were necessary in view of the ever-present dangers in local pits and furnaces although employers did their best to minimise expenditure. The hours of work were long; women worked alongside men, usually at pitheads, and children were employed in the mines as soon as they could prove themselves useful for operating air flaps for ventilation or similar light but exhaustingly repetitive chores, thus helping to increase family income. Formal education was not available to most children.

Fear of unemployment was the key to the power wielded by chartermasters. These were men who operated pits on behalf of the mine or land owner and agreed to extract a given quantity of coal or iron for a specified price. Each chartermaster was expected to provide everything needed to operate the mine, including pit props, picks and ponies. The chartermaster's own profits depended entirely on the ability of his workers to meet his targets; as a consequence, many unreasonable practices became commonplace.

If machinery failed, a pony fell ill or the mine became waterlogged, none of the workers would be paid for 'idle time'. Overtime was seldom paid but often expected in order to meet targets or 'stints'. Industrial disputes, especially when men were told to do work not within their normal remit, were commonplace but workers seldom achieved a worthwhile victory. It was unusual to find a poor chartermaster; they took advantage of their power, cheated their workers and made money in the process.

Another aspect of the chartermasters' regime which caused much ill feeling was their system of operating 'truck' or 'Tommy' shops where essential goods of indifferent quality were sold to workers at abnormally high prices. Towards the end of the eighteenth century, when national small denomination coinage was scarce, mine owners and chartermasters were allowed to produce their own tokens as a substitute for coins of the realm and use them as part payment of wages. These tokens could only be spent in the Tommy shops. Because there were few or no other shops in the vicinity, workers had no choice but to accept the system and pay through the nose. They received their fortnightly pay on a 'Reckoning' Saturday, ate well on Sunday and retired to one of the beer shops on Monday. Work resumed on Tuesday. And so the cycle continued with monotonous regularity. Until a law was passed in 1848 forbidding the unfair practice, wages were sometimes paid in a beerhouse belonging to the chartermaster, who would keep the workers waiting before handing out the wages; in the meantime, the workers were tempted to buy ale. From that time onwards, wages had to be paid in a pit cabin or works building.

Death and incapacity were accepted as hazards of the job. Precautions against roof collapse, fire-damp explosion and even provisions for adequate ventilation were rudimentary. Many deaths were caused simply by exhaustion and carelessness and very few could expect not to be maimed if they worked in or at the mines for any length of time.

Pleasures were of necessity simple; dog and bull baiting, cock-fighting (occasionally organised by the chartermasters for their workers but otherwise enjoyed as part of the Oakengates Wakes) and gambling were commonplace (few were able to read but most could understand the symbols on playing cards and coins). Public hangings at Shrewsbury Gaol were always worth a family outing, despite the long walk if a wagon ride wasn't available; mine owners took it for granted that not much work would be done at such times. Considering public and bank holidays were a rarity, the odd day off for something out of the ordinary was to be expected.

Despite Earl Gower's dislike of alcoholism, drunkenness was rife and added to the problem of safety in the mines. Regardless of the fines and loss of earnings caused by insobriety and late arrival at work, it remained the main means by which the worker, whether man, woman or child, could find release from an oppressive environment.

It is difficult to conceive that such living conditions could be preferable to those elsewhere at that time, but the fact that this was the case gives some indication of the abominable existence led by the less fortunate who toiled in cities like Manchester and Birmingham.

A rare Donnington Wood Glasshouses green glass dog door stop measuring 165mm by 105mm. It was apparently made from the mould of a Coalbrookdale Company cast iron dog with slight adjustment to its base.

Seven
Glass, Grain and Bricks

Donnington Wood Glassworks

The Donnington Wood Glasshouses were situated a couple of hundred metres inside Wrockwardine Wood parish at the western end of the Donnington Wood canal. The glasshouses and the adjacent corn mill are included here solely because they had a close historical connection with Donnington Wood. They are occasionally referred to as the Wrockwardine Wood Glassworks.

Population expansion, transport improvements and the gathering momentum of the industrial revolution, all combined to create an increased demand for glass. William Reynolds, who by the 1780s had a number of coal and iron concerns elsewhere in the district, decided the time was right for erecting a glassworks. His father, Richard, a Quaker married to Abraham Darby's daughter, already had coal mines and iron furnaces in Donnington Wood and had extended the Donnington Wood canal westwards to create the Wombridge Canal in 1788. In 1791, William attempted to form a partnership to open a glassworks with William Phillips, who managed his father's furnaces at Donnington Wood.

The scheme was rejected by William Reynolds' existing partners in the Horsehay Company so, without their support, he and his brother Joseph went into partnership with Phillips anyway in 1792. Raw materials (crushed slag from furnaces, coal, sand, limestone, fireclay and salt) were readily available and the canal assisted transport to the glassworks and subsequent export of finished products from the factory.

Although very little is known about the operation of the works, William was able to count on the considerable expertise gained by his grandfather and father at Bristol and Stourbridge and may well have transferred skilled labour from their own factories. A few of the twenty-five or so glassworkers originally employed definitely came from the Stourbridge area.

The Rectory at Wrockwardine Wood, built during the 1780s and originally the Glassworks' manager's house and works office, has a window pane with 'Donnington Wood Glasshouse August 6th 1792' scratched on its surface. This could well have been the date upon which production began and may even have been the first piece of glass made in the works. This building was purchased by the Church Commissioners in 1847, the same year that Wrockwardine Wood Parish was created.

By 1833 there were two coal-burning furnace cones at the works, a smaller one for producing glass bottles for the Bordeaux wine trade – a 70-gallon bottle was on display to visitors – as well as a wide variety of domestic items (bespeckled jugs, ornamental buttons, rolling pins, door stops in assorted shapes and even twisted striped glass walking sticks). The larger one was probably used to manufacture flat ('broad') window glass. A tax on windows was introduced by the Pitt government in 1794 so it is likely that broad glass manufacture declined soon afterwards; nevertheless, production would have continued to some extent to meet the housing demands in the surrounding area. Furthermore, the Napoleonic war with France severely affected exports; trade was awkward and dangerous. A general recession in the area led to the cessation of coal and iron working for a while and also forced the glassworks to close during 1816, which led to reports of 'a prodigious quantity out of employment and…the parishes are burdened beyond all precedent'. When production recommenced, the emphasis was more towards the manufacture of domestic ware, including black bottles of various shapes and sizes, although the French bottle market could well have resumed.

Richard Mountford, a yeoman from Donnington Wood, was manager of the glassworks by 1796. William Reynolds died in 1803. As his family had no heirs old enough to carry on the business, it was taken over by Richard Mountford in partnership with his brother-in-law William Cope (from Stourbridge), Henry Cope and John Biddle (a chemist from Birmingham who managed an alkali works in Wombridge for William Reynolds). Although this partnership ceased sometime between 1814-1816 when William Cope retired, the others appear to have remained in association for many years; directories for 1821 and 1828 show 'Biddle Mountford & Co.' as having a 'considerable glass manufactory at Donnington Wood'. Pigot's Directory of 1835 shows 'Biddle, Mountford & Cope, glass manufacturers, Donnington Wood'. Cope, Biddle and Mountford also had an interest in a bank at Market Place, Shifnal.

In 1830 a portion of land to the north of the works was donated by its owners, the Earl of Shrewsbury, Lord Berwick and Thomas Spencer, Esq., for the erection of a National School (known by locals as the 'glassus' school) which was built later that year, together with a chapel (now Wrockwardine Wood parish church, built 1833) and a cemetery. The school was originally for girls and infants but later included boys, an indication that continued education for boys was previously considered unnecessary if they were capable of working. The school was enlarged in 1877 to accommodate more infants and again in 1885. It was demolished in 1967.

William Reynolds built several houses for the glasshouse workers (presumably using his own glass in the windows, designed on similar lines to those at Donnington Barracks),

Donnington Wood Glasshouse furnace cones, c. 1833, behind Wrockwardine Wood parish church.

named Glasshouse Row. It seems that some of the glasshouse buildings were converted into dwellings shortly after the factory closed down in 1841 and were called Glasshouse Square. A tithe map of 1847 shows housing at Glasshouse Row (thirty-seven dwellings) and Glasshouse Square (twelve dwellings); the two furnace cones had been demolished by then. Four of the houses backed on to the canal. Each house had small windows in the outer walls, and larger ones to the rear where they overlooked the square and the factory buildings. Entry from the front to the rear was by a small arched gateway just wide enough to allow a cart to pass through. Monday was the traditional day for washing and each household took it in turns to brew beer for their neighbours.

There are no records showing why the business ceased to trade. It must be surmised that changing demands, movement of population and the development of more efficient methods of operation and transport gave rise to factories at other localities.

Biddle and Cope also had glassworks in Birmingham and Stourbridge producing a wide variety of glassware, including cut glass, and must have felt that the Donnington Wood Glasshouses offered limited opportunities for growth. There are indications that the 1838 Glass Duties Act affected glass manufacture and somehow sounded the death knell for the Donnington Wood Glassworks. Excise duty on glass was repealed in 1845, too late to save the business.

Whatever the reasons, the factory suffered a decline during its final years. In 1831 there were sixteen glassworkers living nearby; by the census of 1841, only seven glassworkers remained. Some found alternative employment at St Helens and Stourbridge. In September 1841, Mountford was given notice to quit the premises. He died in January 1842. William Cope was present at his death.

Donnington Wood Flour Mill

The working classes relied heavily on bread in their diets and much rioting came shortly after the cessation of hostilities with France in 1815 when the 'Corn Laws' forced grain prices to soar beyond the reach of ordinary folk. The Donnington Wood Flour Mill Company was established in 1818, near the glassworks on the Wombridge extension to the Donnington Wood Canal, by a partnership comprising John Boycott, John Duncalfe, John Horton and Horton's wife Sarah.

The mill was, to a limited extent, able to alleviate the situation because it supplied corn at a lower price than rivals outside the area. The buildings, which included a baker's oven, were intended to 'carry on business as millers, cornfactors, bakers and dealers in grain'. William Reynolds consulted James Watt on how an engine could be devised to drive two sets of mill stones; he subsequently opened two flour mills in Ketley and Madeley in the 1780s. The same type of engines were installed in the four-storey brick-built Donnington Wood Flour Mill.

Richard Ogle, who became the last manager at the glassworks, was taken into the partnership. John Bullock was the first managing clerk. Between 1818 and 1871, he gradually purchased all shares in the business from the other partners. Thereafter it became known as Bullock's Mill. By 1881 his grandson Thomas employed six men and advertised 'Salopian Glory Flour for best bread and pastry'.

The mill used the western reaches of the canal, which connected to the Trench inclined plane and thence to the Shrewsbury Canal, to transport grain until 1921. The canal was subsequently filled in and made into a pathway but its towpath curb stones are still visible.

The mill continued to be operated by the Bullock family until it was taken over by J.N. Miller & Co. of Wolverhampton in 1943. Production switched from milling flour to grinding animal feed and acting as a depot for distributing grain and cereal to local farmers and other customers. The mill closed in the 1970s.

The Donnington Wood Flour Mill (Bullock's Mill) looking west, c. 1910. Founded in 1818, the mill continued in business alongside part of the Wombridge Canal until the 1970s. The canal linked up with the Donnington Wood Canal a few hundred metres behind the camera. The canal itself has now been filled in and made into a footpath. The children in the photograph were pupils at the nearby 'Glassus' school. The glasshouses themselves were located a few metres to the right.

According to a report in the *Telford Journal* in February 2001, the Mill is destined 'to be transformed into affordable housing, a community room and a police outpost'. Considering the age of the mill and years of dereliction and vandalism, it is encouraging to see steps being taken to preserve the existence of such a landmark.

Brickworks

Almost all the bricks required in the building of dwellings, furnaces and offices were made locally until well into the nineteenth century. The Donnington and Donnington Wood areas had substantial deposits of suitable clay and sand; tithe and old Ordnance Survey maps show several former marl and sand pits as well as brickworks.

Some of the brickworks were very small affairs, which existed for a very short time to meet localised needs and closed soon after the buildings for which they were intended had been erected. Brick making before the beginning of the nineteenth century usually entailed digging clay from the ground, wetting and treading it to render it malleable, throwing it into wooden molds, cutting off the excess with a length of wire and allowing the resulting stacked bricks to dry in temporary open-sided buildings. Small wood- or coal-fired kilns were occasionally used. Badly paid child labour was commonly used.

It was not until the late 1700s that more permanent brickworks were built to cope with an ever-increasing demand for barrack houses, offices, mining and furnace buildings. The Donnington Wood Canal and horse-drawn wagons on tramlines were used to transport the bricks away. With the continued expansion of coal and iron working came excessive quantities of red clay, far greater than was needed locally. Consequently, advantage was taken of the excess to produce red bricks for markets elsewhere (even as far away as Russia) and a new brickworks was built in Donnington Wood in 1850. A siding to the Lilleshall Company's

The Lilleshall Company's Rookery Brickworks.

49

LOT 167.

(Coloured Blue on Plan No. 7.)

An Area of Accommodation Land

With the Well-equipped Premises thereon, hitherto a

Brick and Tile Manufactory,

Yard, and Bed of First-Class Brick Clay

situate at the Fields, Donnington Wood.

In Hand.

THE MANUFACTORY comprises Engine House, Clay Grinding Room, Mixing and Pugging Room, Brick and Tile Making House (66 ft. × 48 ft.), with Drying Pile, Tile and Pipe Making Shed, Drying Shed (60 ft. × 22 ft.), 2 Kilns, each with a capacity for 18,000 Bricks, Circular Kiln, with capacity for 12,000 Bricks, Chimney Stack and Men's Mess Room.

There are also Office, Storehouse, Carpenter's Shop, Stable and Loft.

N.B.—This lot is sold with the reservation that the Purchaser shall not sell to the Public, or place any Bricks, Tiles, Pipes, &c., on the Market.

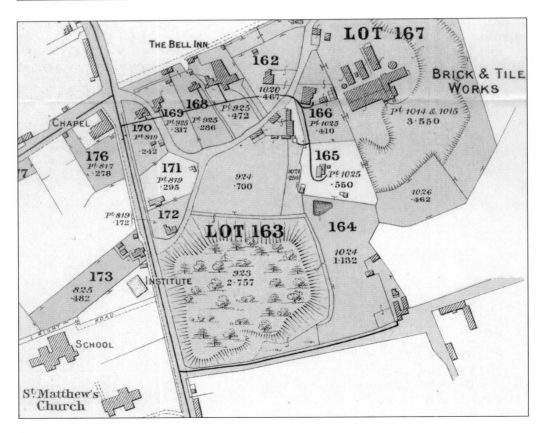

private railway was laid to carry coal from the Grange and Granville Collieries to the brickworks. At that time, bricks were being manufactured under the names Colliery Brickworks, The Rookery Brickworks, White Colliery Brickworks and Woodfield Brickworks.

Working conditions at brickworks, although better than in the mines, were also dangerous. For example, Martha, daughter of Henry Adams (a mine sinker who lived at Donnington Barracks), had one of her hands lopped off while feeding clay rolls into machinery at White Colliery Brickworks in December 1863.

By the 1870s, four brickworks were still in existence; behind The Bell Inn (which also produced tiles and pipes and contained three kilns), near the Old Lodge Furnaces, by Waxhill Barracks (The Woodfield Yard) and at White Colliery near the canal. James and Henry Bourne managed several of them, but whether they were all subsidiaries to a single company is not known. They may well have traded as separate businesses.

However, all of these brickworks appear to have closed down between 1880 and 1901, doubtless affected by the erection of a massive brick and tile works at The Rookery, off St Georges Road, which opened in 1876. This new works was revolutionary in design and was capable of producing considerably greater quantities and varieties of bricks and related products to a higher standard than its predecessors. A brickworks (Wood Brick Kiln) may have existed on the site since about 1800 but this new one surpassed any that had gone before.

Bricks from The Rookery were used in the façade of the Wesleyan Methodist church at Wellington (1881), St Georges Institute and schools at St Georges and Ketley. By 1908 its output reached between three and four million bricks a year. The First World War led to production difficulties with much of the male workforce called up for military service. For the first time, women were employed to fill vacancies. There were seldom more than about forty people employed at The Rookery; most were related and some worked there for between forty and sixty years. This contributed towards a degree of continuity of skills and stability in working relations.

The Rookery Brickworks closed down in 1972; its bricks had become too expensive after the Second World War when architectural and building requirements more frequently demanded bricks of a lower quality.

The brickwork premises behind The Bell Inn were sold as part of the Duke of Sutherland Lilleshall Estate sale in July 1914. One of the stipulations of the sale was that whoever purchased the property would not sell any bricks, tiles or pipes to the public, presumably because it would be in direct competition with The Rookery works. The buildings had been demolished by the early 1920s.

Opposite: *Particulars and detail from a plan in the 1914 catalogue for the sale of the Duke of Sutherland's Lilleshall Estate, showing the location of the Brick and Tile Works behind The Bell Inn. Lots 162 and 166 were once 'The Flag' and 'The Boot' public houses. Lot 163 comprised The Bell Inn together with several outbuildings, a field and the partly wooded Black Bank opposite the church Institute (not to be confused with the Mechanics Institute on the Bell Field). The chapel adjacent to Lot 176 (W.H. Mason's butcher's shop) was the original Baptist church, built in 1820, on the corner of Queens Road and Church Road. The school was St Matthew's National School.*

The Freehold Pit, c. 1920. Being the lowest-lying pit in the area, it had a dreadful reputation for flooding, so much so that miners frequently had to work waist high in filthy, freezing water. The land immediately north of the hill top site is now known as Muxton Marsh, reflecting the high water table in relation to the surrounding area. The mine shaft was used as a tip for obsolete and surplus equipment by the COD after the Second World War.

The Granville Colliery pithead in 1944; extensive rebuilding followed nationalisation in 1947.

Eight
The Nineteenth Century

The year 1802 saw the formation of the Lilleshall Company partnership, which succeeded the Leveson Gower partnership with the Gilbert brothers. Almost straight away it took control over all mining in Donnington Wood. One of the new partners was John Bishton, who had become the Marquis of Stafford's agent on the Lilleshall estates in 1788 and who already had several iron-making interests in the area, all of which came under the control of the partnership on his death in 1807. It was largely due to Bishton's influence that the Leveson Gowers became involved in the iron trade, beginning with the erection of further furnaces at the Old Lodge in Donnington Wood, which were served by a short cutting to the main canal.

The composition of the Lilleshall Company changed frequently between 1802 and 1813 as partners died, others were bought out and new members introduced. Eventually it included William Horton, who, with his son John, were prominent figures in the activities of the company during the century.

The Napoleonic Wars gave rise to a great demand for iron which continued until 1812 when the ensuing peace caused a dramatic decline in the Shropshire iron trade. In 1806 a ton of forge pig iron was worth £6 15s, in 1812 £5 10s, and by 1816, £3 15s. Acute depression followed, many mines and furnaces were closed and unemployment rose sharply. Other areas, such as South Wales and the Black Country, soon dominated the iron trade owing to their ability to employ more efficient production methods and a more favourable geographical position in relation to new areas of demand. The Lilleshall Company was the only Shropshire partnership to maintain a satisfactory standard of production and, in fact, increased its operations until, by 1815, it controlled most of the industrial activities in this northern part of the Coalbrookdale coalfield.

The area's first deep mine, opened to exploit richer seams to the east, was sunk at Waxhill Barracks in 1818, followed by the Muxtonbridge mine in 1837. The Freehold mine may have begun operations shortly after 1840 and the Granville Colliery started sinking between 1854 and 1860. In 1857, sparks from the Granville pithead chimney caused a fire in the stockyard at Muxton Grange belonging to Farmer Dawes. Water from the canal was used to douse burning barley and wheat and over £500 worth of damage was caused. In May 1860, church bells were rung at Wellington and Lilleshall to celebrate the sinking of a shaft at the Granville mine and the discovery of a metre-thick seam of coal reckoned to be 100m wide stretching eastwards. Grange colliery opened in 1864 (in its early years it was known locally as the Albert and Alexandra pit).

Barn Pit and Meadow Pit opened during the mid-nineteenth century but several mines were closed down and others linked together below ground in an effort to improve safety by providing an alternative escape route in case disaster struck. A few privately run pits (like Poppit's and Hewlett's) were allowed to survive until they were no longer economic or their leases expired.

Tokens and checks from an industrial past. Top row: Salop Miners Association and Federation membership tokens. Second row: Safety Checks for the Freehold, Muxtonbridge, Lodge and Donnington Pits. Third row: Lamp Checks used at the Lilleshall Company's Granville Pits before nationalisation. Fourth row: Lamp Checks allocated to miners working at the Granville Colliery after the National Coal Board took over operations in 1947. The Granville Pits were also known as the Lilleshall Colliery. Bottom row, left: Two Checks issued to workers at C & W Walker's Midland Iron Works. The earlier one on the left was produced with a laurel wreath motif on the reverse. Later checks had blank reverses. Bottom row, right: Two Checks issued to workers at the Lilleshall Company's Rookery (Donnington) Brickworks. Each worker was allocated two checks (one containing holes) with the same number. One check was used to record daily attendance at the brickworks; the other was used to identify workers collecting their wages.

The chartermaster system continued throughout the century despite frequent criticism of its injustices. William Clemson, Moses Martin, Thomas Mainwaring, Thomas Ward and John Woodvine were some of the chartermasters still working pits during the mid-nineteenth century, as were John Woodvine and Joseph Dorricott. The latter were successfully sued (a very rare occurrence) by Margaret and Elizabeth Lloyd for wages amounting to 5s 6d owed to them. Chartermasters liked to make money but not pay out. Grocer William Wright of Wellington sued Mr Ball of Donnington Wood in 1857 because Ball owed him £3 17s for candles. On the other hand, workers could be sued by their chartermaster if they failed to give sufficient notice to quit; Thomas Blayney received 9s 6d from George and John Shingler, both of whom had left his pit in 1855 in search of work in Staffordshire.

Even though the Duke of Sutherland was patently made aware of the situation after Chartists went on strike in 1842 and a public enquiry followed, no attempt was made to put an end to the chartermaster system. (In fact, Mr Cooper, the last chartermaster to operate at the Granville Colliery, operated until his retirement in 1913 at which time the practice ceased.) Further unrest in 1842 led to the arrest of several miners who were charged with rioting, including Thomas Bould, John Brothwood, Moses Stanworth and Thomas Williams.

Safety in the mines was not something to which chartermasters or mine owners paid too much attention. They followed common sense practices up to a point but regular inspections of ropes and equipment were not carried out as frequently as they should have been; this is evident from inquest reports into mining deaths. Nevertheless, as time went by, miners' lamps replaced bare candlelight. Lamp checks (also called tokens, tickets and passes) were introduced during the 1860s and continued until 1979, although their use was not compulsory until 1913.

The method of using these tokens, which resembled small coins and contained the mine name and a number allocated to each worker, varied from pit to pit. Sometimes the worker exchanged his token for a lamp engraved with the same number. In other pits, the same was done but the miner had a duplicate token which was kept in his pocket during the shift. Other pits followed different procedures but the object of the exercise was the same; the managers needed to know exactly who was working inside the mine at any given time in case there was a disaster. The Lilleshall Company used similar tokens in their offices and factories as well as the mines as a check on attendance and for identifying workers collecting wages.

Despite short periods when output fell, the overall trend was decidedly upwards. More furnaces were erected at the Old Lodge in 1846 and 1859 to supplement those already working until, by 1871, when the famous Henry Bessemer (inventor of a revolutionary process of iron smelting) visited them, there were nine furnaces. Eight of these were almost constantly in action, producing 1,400 tons of pig iron each week. Nearby some fifty ovens prepared coke from the local coal, and engine sheds, rolling mills and forges transformed the pig iron into saleable ware.

By the mid-1840s there were over forty pits in Donnington Wood raising about 100,000 tons of coal each year and roughly 50,000 tons of ironstone, according to contemporary sources. In 1871 production had risen to 400,000 tons of coal and 105,000 tons of ironstone. Although there had been a reduction in the number of mines since the late eighteenth century, those which remained or were newly created operated more efficiently; output continued to grow and it is largely because of activities in this period that the landscape was almost completely denuded of its ancient woodland and replaced by numerous spoil heaps, some of which still remain. Thriving brick and tile works also contributed to the desolation. It was not until the second half of the century that the Duke of Sutherland felt obliged to implement a small amount of afforestation; one of the areas to benefit from tree planting was the Black Bank opposite St Matthew's church. By 1846, supplies of suitable limestone at Lilleshall were exhausted and new supplies had to be transported from other areas, such as Wenlock Edge and Steeraway near Wellington. The shallower coal beds were also becoming exhausted, but improved mining safeguards and machinery enabled deeper seams to be exploited.

Donnington railway station, looking westwards, late 1950s. The approaching train from Wellington is on its way to Stafford via Newport and Gnosall. C & W Walker's 'turret' clock, refurbished and repainted, now stands on top of a small brick tower on a roundabout approximately where the station buildings once stood. The present A518 Wellington-Newport road follows the course of the railway line.

The gigantic Lodge Furnaces at Donnington Wood as illustrated in S. Griffiths' Guide to the Iron Trade, 1873. The furnaces were finally blown out in 1888 and allowed to fall into decay.

By far the greatest impetus to coal and iron production at that time was the development of steam power, not only as a means of driving factory and mining equipment but also the steam engine as a means of transportation, which had enormous social and economic repercussions. Until the railway line passed through Donnington in June 1849, and a link made to the collieries, the transport system was dominated by the canals, supplemented by iron tramways and roads like the main Wellington-Newport Turnpike Road.

The Shropshire Union Railway (SUR) was formed in which George Granville Leveson Gower, the second Duke of Sutherland (his father George Granville Leveson Gower had been created Duke shortly before his death in 1833) was a partner. The station at Donnington almost immediately caused a decline in the traffic on the turnpike road and – perhaps more importantly – on the canal. The Donnington Wood Canal managed to survive for several decades but virtually the whole ceased to be used commercially on Christmas Day, 1882. Strong competition between the various railway companies in Shropshire during their formative years led to drastic reductions in freight charges; many, including the SUR, were taken over by larger companies, so that by 1854 only two, the Great Western and the London-North West, controlled all commercial railways on the coalfield.

The prosperous years of the third quarter of the century were short-lived for the iron trade. By the 1880s most ironworks on the coalfield suffered a decline of unprecedented proportions, due mainly to competition from Staffordshire, severe economic depression and a failure to adopt modern methods of production. Although iron reserves were plentiful, extraction became uneconomic; iron processing continued but the companies which survived the years of depression concentrated more on semi-finished iron for Black Country factories; the Lilleshall Company was again the one exception to the general trend. In 1880 the partnership altered its status to that of a limited company and made comprehensive changes to its management and production systems.

The Lodge Furnaces were blown out in 1888 and from then on the company concentrated its operations at Snedshill and the New Yard at St Georges. Priorslee Hall was the headquarters of the company for many years and home of its managing director until it was purchased by Telford Development Corporation in the late 1960s. Donnington Wood was no longer an important iron production area but, despite continued coal activities and the growth of C & W Walker lron Works at Donnington, wages fell to a level lower than could be obtained in the newer centres of manufacturing industry. The railways made movement of population easier and furthered the decline of Donnington Wood by encouraging migration to higher-paid employment elsewhere.

Although most of the land in Donnington remained in the possession of the Lilleshall Company until the late 1930s, its economic concerns did not effectively stretch beyond the mines, apart from providing jobs at Snedshill and the New Yard.

Throughout the first three-quarters of the century the population grew steadily; by 1881 there were 1,871 people living in 326 dwellings in the whole of the Donnington-Donnington Wood area. Overcrowding was a perpetual problem but still preferable to the squalid conditions elsewhere as the nation's populace became more urbanised.

The employment of children continued; boys as young as eight worked in abominable conditions for pitiful pay. In 1812, John Holmes and William Adams were paid two shillings for twenty-four days work; Richard Attwood was paid 1s 9d while Samuel Bloor received 1s 4d. Others were paid more, some less. Boys became men from the age of thirteen years and could eventually expect to receive high wages. Given that many women bore a child every two years, families of between five and ten children were common. Even though infant mortality was high, those who survived afforded the possibility of adding income to the family budget as well as providing support during their parents' declining years.

If they were lucky and their parents could afford it, a few youngsters – mainly boys but sometimes girls – were taken on as apprentices to learn such trades as wheelwrighting, joinery, carpentry, building, blacksmithing, pattern making, moulding and puddling. Some became shoemakers and tailors. Parents paid an 'incentive' to the craftsman who sometimes took the child into his home and expected to pay virtually nothing during the full term of the apprenticeship, which could last for up to ten years. It was not until later in the century that apprentices did not need to pay a consideration in order to gain employment and instead were actually paid while learning the trade. If they weren't employed at the mines, girls tended to go into service or, later in the century, obtain employment in shops at Wellington and Oakengates.

The Marquis of Stafford and his descendants the Dukes of Sutherland eased social shortcomings to some extent by expelling the perpetrators of the housing problem – the 'middlemen'. By 1820 the Leveson Gowers had made the cottagers their immediate tenants and took an active interest in their well-being. Regular surveys were made and good tenants rewarded with grants of land for the keeping of livestock (usually one or two cattle, pigs and chickens). Subsidence-damaged houses were repaired or demolished and new dwellings built, most of them near the Old Yard (a vague term relating to the area along the canal a few hundred yards south of where St Matthew's church stands and stretching to both sides of St Georges Road). Whether the Leveson Gowers' interest was purely philanthropic is a matter for debate; it seems more likely that decent housing was intended to encourage more responsible attitudes both to work and social life. In any event, a fair proportion of money paid to workers as wages was recovered in rent.

A survey in the 1850s revealed that twenty out of twenty-seven dwellings at Waxhill Barracks had more than five inhabitants living in their allocated two rooms; several had nine or more living in them. As a result of the survey, the Duke authorised the conversion of disused furnaces, engine-houses, etc., into workers' dwellings. Again, this decision meant more income from rent could be derived from properties which would otherwise fall further

Pumping engine at Stephens' Pit, situated on the Donnington Wood Canal a few yards south of St Matthew's church. The chartermaster, George Richard Stephens, stands second from the right. The pit ceased operations before 1880 but continued to pump water into the canal, to help drain surrounding mines, until 1928.

into disrepair and lose value. Stipulations on the design of permanent office buildings at C & W Walker's were also made so that they could be converted into dwellings if the company folded. (In the event, when the company ceased operations in Donnington, the buildings were demolished.)

This period also saw the erection of 'Sutherland' cottages with their distinctive gable ends. They were built to a common plan, presumably to keep architect's fees in check, and could be varied according to need. They were built not only in the Donnington-Lilleshall area but also in other parts of the family's Shropshire estates.

Until the development of Local Government, the welfare of the populace and upkeep of civic facilities (such as roads and housing) rested with the local gentry, who regarded such matters as a traditional responsibility. The Leveson Gowers maintained a paternalistic interest throughout the nineteenth century and in difficult times (such as the post-war and other depressions) found alternative employment on the farms, timber-felling in the woods, afforestation of denuded pit mounds and road and bridge repair, so that the burden on the Poor Law Authorities was to some extent reduced. It also kept idle hands occupied and maintained rental income.

Several charities, such as Queen Anne's Bounty, Lady Katherine's Bounty, T.E. Horton's Charity and further combined funds founded by the Duke, his son Earl Granville and T.E. Horton of the Lilleshall Company, provided small annual sums for the benefit of widows, the aged and infirm as well as the poor.

Benefit clubs began, funded by subscriptions from labourers; these were the forerunners of the present trades unions. In those days it was rare for any worker to save much money; banks were unreliable and regarded with suspicion, and the cost of living relatively high in relation to wages. Starvation could be an important factor in forcing miners back to work after striking against reductions in wages, as happened in 1821, 1865 and 1876. Nevertheless, benefit clubs provided a form of insurance in the event of death at work.

Workers tried to supplement their wages with every capable person in the family working, but as the century progressed various Acts of Parliament forbade the employment of young children and restricted hours of work. Even as late as 1874, the Duke was fined for permitting infants to work in his brick-kilns, a fact which tends to confirm that he (and, by association, the Lilleshall Company) did not care so much about working conditions but rather wished to keep wages down to a minimum.

Women continued to do back-breaking menial work, although some were employed in semi-skilled jobs, such as operating pithead machinery, for which they received the title 'engineer'. Part-time work, like shop-keeping, odd-jobbing and animal husbandry, were increasingly undertaken in an effort to increase income. In the closing years of the century, a few enterprising souls began embryonic public transport services using a horse and cart to carry people to the markets at Wellington and Oakengates.

Divisions began to appear between the working classes. Those attending church services and Sunday schools did so two or three times on the Sabbath and tried to follow the scriptures, save what little money they could and bring their children up to live decent lives. Those who preferred drinking, gambling and the temptations of the flesh were regarded as outcasts, only to be tolerated in the working environment. Domestic violence and public disorder were to be expected. In 1857, John Bate was charged with assaulting his wife. In the same year, labourer William Hoof of Donnington and Thomas Palmer of Trench were charged with breach of the peace and Samuel Taylor, a tailor at Donnington, was sentenced to fourteen days in prison for being found drunk and disorderly in Oakengates.

Some people turned to crime. Theft was frequent. Stealing of coal to heat perpetually damp dwellings was commonplace but few were caught; George Thomas was apprehended in March 1824. Peter Rigby, who apparently had a 'weak intellect', was apprehended for theft of coal in April 1867. Thomas Bishton was transported in 1834 for stealing a top coat and other articles from a house in Donnington. In 1838, John Griffiths (a known offender) was transported for seven years for stealing £2 3s from John Worrall's house, as was William Charles who stole clothes from the home of Benjamin Phillips. In 1841 Thomas Simms assaulted Benjamin Nicholls and stole £50 worth of silver intended to pay wages at Donnington Wood Furnaces. Simms was also transported. In August 1867, William Bould stole tools from C & W Walker's works.

A highway robbery occurred at Waxhill Barracks in February 1857 when William Martin and William Icke stole from Thomas Hughes and Robert Jones. John Houghton tried to make off with 10cwt of cast iron tram rails belonging to the Lilleshall Company but was caught taking them in his cart for sale at Shrewsbury. In March 1857, Ann Hoof was sentenced to seven days in prison by magistrate Sir John Charlton (of Apley Castle) for stealing a cape from a Mrs Campbell of Wolverhampton while attending Oakengates Market.

Theft of food, especially during periods of unemployment, was very common. Whereas anyone with an ounce of commonsense would pick crops from fields at night, some deserved to be caught, as was William Fewtrell who received three months hard labour for stealing a quantity of wheat from the Donnington Wood Mill.

Assaults and attempted murder also cropped up from time to time, such as in 1855 when Robert Jones was seen strangling fifteen-year-old Solomon Fryer to death in a hut near The Bell Inn. Jones was released because witnesses were deemed unreliable. In 1856 Joseph Brothwood alias Proudler, a notorious character, assaulted Joseph Nicholls' wife. He chose the wrong victim; Joseph Nicholls was the parish police constable at Trench.

The former Boot Inn, c. 1910. It was included as Lot 166 in the Lilleshall Estate sale catalogue of 1914. The property was purchased by the tenant, Mr D. Robinson, for £190.

Others turned to home-brewing (despite the Duke's support of the Temperance League) and two opened inns – the 'Flag' and the 'Boot', which were situated behind the 'Bell'. The 'Boot' was forced to close for a while in 1878 because it had gained an unsavoury reputation for encouraging the wiles of fallen women. There is no record of when the 'Flag' ceased to trade, probably towards the end of the century or when the nearby brickworks closed down. It, too, had gained an unsavoury reputation.

The Bell Inn, which had a consistently good reputation among locals for most of its life, was granted a seven-day license in 1896 when Mary Nicholls was the occupier, although it first opened for business some time before 1800. It originally had stables for visitors' horses. The publican in 1855 was John Nicholls; his son, Joseph Nicholls became the publican on his father's death a year later. It has been suggested that The Bell relates to an earlier time when local news was dispensed by someone who rang a bell to attract attention (a bit like a town crier) but this is unlikely. Another theory put forward is that income derived from the adjacent field was allocated to maintain the bell at Lilleshall church, a practice common throughout England at the time. However, fieldname maps do not support this view. It is possible that the name simply reflects the old practice of digging bell-shaped pits in the vicinity.

The original Sutherland Arms in Donnington may have originated as an eighteenth-century coaching house. Its publican in 1896, when there was still stabling for eleven horses, was Uriah Pearce. All the pubs were owned by the Duke of Sutherland as part of the Lilleshall Estate. Both The Bell Inn and Sutherland Arms were used to store corpses and conduct post mortem enquiries after mining and other industrial deaths.

Centre of sporting and cultural activities for many years: The Bell Inn, c. 1910.

Donnington Wood.

LOT 163.

(Coloured Green on Plan No. 7.)

The well situated

Fully Licensed Public House

KNOWN AS

"THE BELL INN," DONNINGTON WOOD

*Tenant :—*Mr. J. Lees.

THIS WIDELY KNOWN HOUSE is situated in a thickly populated industrial District and does an excellent trade ; the accommodation is as follows : Smoke Room, (15 ft. by 10 ft.), Tap Room (19 ft. by 11 ft. 6 ins.), Club Room (24 ft. by 13 ft. 6 ins.), Sitting Room (31 ft. x 10 ft. 6 ins.), Bar, Kitchen, Pantry, Cellar, Scullery, 4 Bedrooms and Small Room.

Adjoining are Brew-house, Small Store, 2 Cellars.

THE OUTBUILDINGS comprise : Saddle Room and Loose Box with Loft, 4 Pigsties and Boiling House, Two-stall Stable and Loft, Trap House and Loose box with Loft over, Fowl-House.

There is a good Field of Pasture Land ; nicely laid out Garden well stocked with fruit trees.

The Summit of the Mound is grassed over with Vetch, Trefoil and Clover, the sides are planted with a large variety of Ornamental and Timber Trees, which are in a very thriving state ; from the top extensive and beautiful views are obtained, and with little difficulty a Bowling Green could be made thereon.

Gas and Water are laid on.

This Lot is sold subject to the Right of the existing Pipe Line and of access thereto, in connection with the Water Works, as shown on Plan.

Apportioned Annual Rental £80 10s. 0d.

Particulars of The Bell Inn included in the Lilleshall Estate sale catalogue of 1914. Jim Lees, the sitting tenant, purchased the whole Lot for £2,350, a substantial sum reflecting both trading success and the amount of land included. Jim Lees was highly respected, not only by his regulars but also the local community for the support he gave to sporting and cultural activities. His catering skills were second to none; he was frequently called on to provide marquee refreshment at the Oakengates Wakes as well as for important celebrations in the Donnington area.

Leisure activities gradually altered in response to the influence of various religious movements and changing moral values. Heavy drinking and blood sports were discouraged and pastimes like brass bands gained popularity, as they did in other mining areas. Working class women were largely ignored when it came to entertainment; their place was at home.

The Donnington Wood Institute Brass Band was formed around 1851 and met for rehearsals at the Mechanics Institute, a wooden building near The Bell Inn; the building itself was erected or replaced around 1867 and had a small supply of books for the education of its members. More people could read as a result of the Education Acts twenty years earlier.

Before long the band attained a standard of performance suitable for public appearances. In September 1856 it played at a 'pleasure party' in the grounds of Lilleshall Abbey, travelling there in tub boats on the canal. By 1859 it was performing at important functions and led a procession for the Earl Granville Lodge of the Oddfellows Friendly Society in Oakengates. It also led the main procession at St Georges for public celebrations of the Prince of Wales' marriage to Alexandra of Denmark in March 1863. The band was in great demand not only for outdoor processions and performances but also for indoor concerts, at this time led by John Bradley.

The Bell Fields, c. 1960. The railway line to the Granville Colliery cuts across the top of the photograph. Coronation Drive can be seen on the left and the Black Bank to the right, opposite St Matthew's church. By this time, the square-shaped pavillion, football fields, tennis courts, swimming and paddling pools, etc., were all under local council control. Some of the oldest remaining dwellings in Donnington Wood lie on either side of the road which curves around The Bell Inn, whose car park can be seen to the right of the tennis courts, bottom centre.

Donnington.
LOT 95.

(Coloured Green on Plan No. 3).

A well Situated and Valuable

Fully Licensed Public House

KNOWN AS

" THE SUTHERLAND ARMS "

TOGETHER WITH THE

Premises, Farm Buildings, Cottage and 23 Acres of Good Arable and Pasture Land.

Tenant :—Mr. J. H. PEARCE.

THE HOUSE contains good accommodation as follows :—Entrance Hall, good Sitting Room (16ft. by 12ft. 6in.), Dining Room (17ft. by 14ft.), Work Room, Bar, Smoke Room and Tap Room, Kitchen, Good Dairy and Store Room, Large Cellar and 5 good Bedrooms.

There is a very convenient Brewhouse & Bakehouse, also a Lawn & good Garden well stocked with Fruit Trees.

Gas and Water are laid on.

THE BUILDINGS comprise good Cowshed for 12, Store Cattle Shed, 2 Loose Boxes, Stabling for 5 Horses, Foaling Box, Three-bay Cart Shed, 2 Implement Sheds, Fowl House, 3 Workshops, Trap House, Trap Shed, Root and Mixing House with Fodder Loft, Granary, Fodder Lofts.

COTTAGE and GARDEN

Sub-Tenant :— CARTWRIGHT.

THE LAND is of good sound quality and extends to 23 Acres ; a further Area of 16¼ Acres hatched Green on Plan (see Tenancy Schedule below), which is included in the present Tenancy at a Yearly Rental of £24 18s. 4d., but which is not included in the Sale, is open to be taken by the Purchaser of this Lot by arrangement on a yearly Tenancy, subject to the usual Estate Agreement, and providing the Purchaser expresses his desire in writing within three months of the date of Sale, to take the Land.

"THE SUTHERLAND ARMS" is situate adjoining the main road in a populous district and is the only Public House of any kind within a radius of about a mile, and is within a short distance of the Midland Iron Works and Donnington Railway Station.

TIMBER :—Included with the Freehold of this Lot is the Timber standing thereon, estimated to have a value of £7 10s. 0d.

The Sutherland Arms, c. 1910 and Particulars included in the Lilleshall Estate sale catalogue of 1914. The sitting tenant, J.H. Pearce, purchased the property for £3,400.

Unfortunately, a crisis arose in 1868 when the band was asked to become the official band of the Shropshire Rifle Volunteers. Several key members who wished to take up the offer left to form a new band based at the Barley Mow Inn, St Georges, a township which already had a respected band. The breakaway band even placed this advertisement in the Wellington Journal in May 1869: 'The celebrated Donnington Wood Brass Band can be engaged for fetes, anniversaries, harvest homes &c. All the newest and best music of the day, including that played at the Queens Birthday. For terms, apply to J. Smith, Gower Street, St Georges, W.H. Smith, Boot Inn, Donington or S. Turner, Wrockwardine Wood.'! One of their number, William Henry Smith, ran the Boot Inn. Feelings against him ran so high that trade rapidly decreased, so much so that Smith felt obliged to close the pub and move away from the district.

Mr Tart set about restoring the fortunes of the original band. By 1870 it was performing in public again, but another crisis arose in 1875 when depression hit industry in the area. Many people left in search of work elsewhere, so the Donnington Wood and one of the St Georges' bands decided to join forces when occasion demanded. Several of the St Georges men made up the numbers for the Donnington Wood Band at events such as the School Treat and Summer Festival at Beckbury village hall in 1883. Every penny earned helped the players and their families in these hard times. Food was just as important as money and several bandsmen were observed slipping food from the tables into their empty instrument cases to feed their families when they returned home.

Because of falling numbers and a growing reluctance to continue association with any of the bands at St Georges, the Donnington Wood Brass Band was obliged to disband in 1897 and store all its instruments at The Bell Inn until the situation improved.

Life was still difficult despite a gradual improvement in living conditions. Adequate sanitation was not provided until the institution of District and Parish Councils at the end of the century. The amount of concern shown by the Ironmasters reflected the state of the economy.

The post-Napoleonic War depression reached its lowest point between 1818 and 1821; reductions in wages resulted in widespread strikes. About 400 colliers broke into the Donnington Wood furnaces causing considerable damage and the yeomanry at Wellington (the peace-keeping force before the police) were called out to quell the riots. It was partly because of this that the Leveson Gowers took greater interest in the welfare of their workers; the erection of a monument on Lilleshall Hill in memory of the first Duke of Sutherland was paid for by (apparently) voluntary subscriptions of his tenants and is a testimony to the appreciation felt for his efforts. Attitudes on the family's Scottish estates in Sutherland tell a different story, where sheep seemed more important than the people who were cleared ruthlessly off the land.

There were several trade recessions in later years when wages again had to be reduced, but the resulting strikes were not so violent as those in 1821. Conditions in the mines were still dangerous towards the end of the century and deaths and accidents were frequent, although the denial of child labour and the enforcement of shorter working hours helped to ease the problem.

Cattle plague was prevalent in the 1860s and drastically affected the supply of fresh meat. A general lack of hygiene led to outbreaks of scarlet fever and smallpox during the 1870s and 1880s. The erection of a small wooden hospital in 1883 came too late to be of any use and soon closed.

One aspect of the nineteenth century which cannot be over-emphasised is the effect death had, not just on the immediate family but also the whole community.

Death lurked in every corner, it struck in all manner of ways. Disease, canal drowning (twenty-one-year-old Joseph Poppitt, who suffered from fits, fell into the canal and drowned in 1864; a similar fate met a child named Noah Latham three years later), falling into pits (a twenty-year-old woman fell 190 yards to her death in October 1864), breaking chains (three men killed in June 1875), explosions, gassing and burning (as happened to Thomas Brothwood in 1847 and someone named Rushton a year later) and rock falls – all were to be expected. Some deaths were simply unfortunate; for example, a Mr Hayward was pulling down a wall at Waxhill Barracks in 1867. He tossed one of the bricks away, accidentally killing a child. John Luter witnessed an accident in November 1870 when William Richards, a slack washer at Lodge Furnaces, was bringing in a laden truck pulled along the tramway by a horse. The truck began moving faster than the horse; Richards became entangled in the chains and couldn't pull on the brake quickly enough. He was crushed against a stationery truck further along the tramway and later died of his wounds. His inquest at The Bell Inn was attended by Dr George McCarthy.

Thomas Hatfield and Mr Corfield died in pits in 1819. Five boys were killed in a pit in 1821; Miss Bolan died at Hewlett's Pit in 1842. A year earlier, John Hewlett, the chartermaster, was drawn over the pulley at the pit and killed; the event was witnessed by his engineer, Henry Cooper, and Sarah Edge, one of his workers. In 1859, chartermaster Sheppard had almost reached the bottom of his pit shaft when the crank of the engine snapped and the weight of a falling loaded skip drew up Mr Sheppard 'at a frightful speed'. His head struck the pithead equipment, slashing into his face as far back as his ears, before his body was catapulted a hundred yards into a field. His son had died at the pit some fourteen months earlier; Sheppard's grief-stricken widow was committed to the asylum in Shrewsbury. In 1863, Thomas Southall was killed in a pit chartered by James Broxton for the Lilleshall Company. Southall left a widow and five children. Henry Johnson was killed in a firedamp explosion at Granville Pit; Thomas Rider and Enoch Horton miraculously survived. Another man who must have counted his blessings was Richard Oliver; about a ton of coal fell on him in 1867 while he was working in a pit chartered by John Taylor; he survived.

In December 1894, twenty-four-year-old Alice Fryer, a maid serving in Eccles, was on her way home to spend Christmas with her parents George and Hannah at Donnington Wood. The Manchester-London train she was travelling on was hit by a shunting wagon blown into its path by strong winds; forty-three perished and over a hundred were injured. Alice is buried in St Matthew's churchyard. Chronic respiratory diseases, specifically related to mining, became more frequent as the century progressed (indeed, claims are still being made against the National Coal Board over twenty years after mining ceased in Donnington Wood in 1979). Drunkenness also played a part as did general fatigue from working excessively long hours.

The list of fatalities throughout the century was long. Many resulted in public displays of sympathy and enormous crowds attended funerals. Resentment against chartermasters was constant, particularly as the question of compensation for the death of employees seldom arose. Small sums, sometimes no more than five pounds, were occasionally offered to grieving relatives as an act of goodwill. Donations from ordinary folk attending funerals could be many times greater.

The most terrible mining disaster in Donnington Wood took place in 1875 at Lodgebank colliery in the Old Lodge area. Eleven men were overcome by fumes when they were lowered into the mine to start work. A pit pony was then lowered in chains to join them; it died while still in its harness before reaching the bottom of the shaft. The courage of the men sent down afterwards to recover the bodies cannot be imagined, particularly since the cause of death was not known until afterwards. One by one the bodies were brought out and carried away to their separate homes by grieving relatives. Thereafter the pit was known as the Slaughter Pit. (*Death and Disaster in Victorian Telford*, by the same author, gives further details of this and other mining disasters.)

The coming of the railways brought new opportunities to visit other towns and generally improved communications; however, they also caused a decline in the use of roads (the

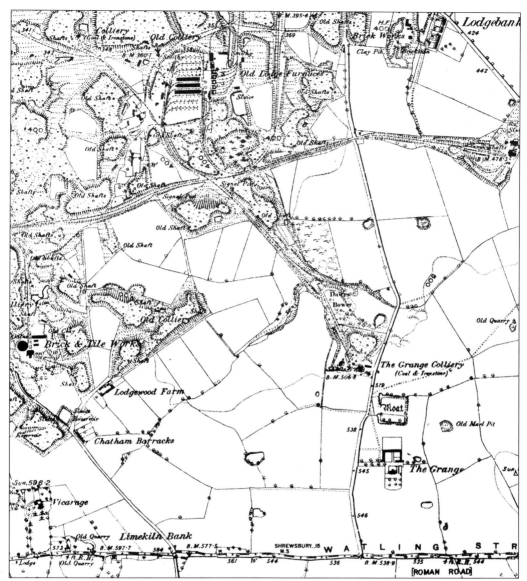

The south of Donnington Wood as detailed in an Ordnance Survey map, 1889. Granville Colliery lies immediately south of Lodgebank, top right. The old Lodge Furnace rail network can be seen surrounding and entering the furnace area; the furnaces themselves had ceased production a year earlier. Centre left is the newly-built circular Rookery Brick and Tile Works. Chatham Barracks, like Donnington Barracks, housed Lilleshall Company workers, some of whom may have been employed at Grange Colliery. As with the rest of Donnington Wood, there are many old clay and marl pits and quarries as well as coal pit shafts although it is extremely unlikely that they had all been identified; doubtless there were countless more buried beneath the widespread spoil heaps.

Lilleshall Toll Gate was taken down in 1867 after several years of running at a loss).

Markets at Wellington, Oakengates and elsewhere were visited more frequently and a new leisure-time activity developed – excursions to seaside resorts and trips to see relatives in other areas. Gone were the days when people rarely travelled far from their homes and places of work. When trade in the Donnington area declined during the closing years of the century, the railway network assisted the migration of workers to other centres where industry was prospering. The Donnington of 1900 seemed set to slide into a state of decay.

Lines on the sad accident at the Donnington Wood Colliery, Shropshire on Saturday September 11th, 1875.

Pray listen to these reeling verses,
Which we now relate to you,
At Donnington and miles around it
There is much grief and misery too
For eleven poor hard working colliers
Went to labour under ground
But by fire in the coal mine,
A dreadful death they all have found.

It was at Donnington Wood in Shropshire
These poor colliers under ground
By a fire in the coal mine,
A dreadful death they all have found.

To their work that fatal morning
These poor souls their way did wend
Little dreaming, little thinking,
They'd meet with such a sudden end.
Down the shaft they all descended -
To labour for their daily bread
And very soon it was discovered,
That these poor colliers were all dead.

Some men both willing and brave hearted
To save the sufferers then did try
They risk'd their lives to search the workings
And a fearful sight there met their eye,
Men who went down strong and healthy
Now were found to be quite dead,
All their troubles they were ended
And their spirits they had fled.

Some poor men and women assembled
When the sad tidings they were known
Friends were looking for their comrades
Relations looking for their own
And when they brought up their dead bodies
The sight was grievous to behold
The anguish of their wives and neighbours
No tongue can tell or pen unfold.

The dangers that surround poor colliers
God in heaven only knows
He ne'er is certain of returning
When down beneath the ground he goes.
We hope their souls are now in heaven
From their labour now at rest
We hope they're happy with the angels
And by their loving Saviour blest.

Contemporary ballad relating to the Donnington Wood pit disaster, 1875.

Nine

From 1900 to 1939

The twentieth century saw the relatively speedy substitution of the Leveson Gowers' traditional patronage with the rise in importance of local government councils. There were three types of council created by Acts of Parliament in an effort to institute effective government throughout the country and to take charge of all civic matters affecting the community.

Parish councils dealt with problems at a local level and were responsible to a district council, which provided them with financial support and decided policies of reform for the area. The district councils were controlled by a single county council. The basic system of local government has altered little since it began, although its powers and influence have been increased over the years by further Acts of Parliament. Donnington and Lilleshall are sub-divisions ('wards') of the Lilleshall Parish Council which was appointed in 1894, when it had seven representatives.

The council at that time depended to a degree upon the goodwill of the Duke of Sutherland and the Lilleshall Company to improve civic amenities as they were still landlords of much of the area, and the council had very limited powers of enforcement. The Duke assisted the council in such matters as the laying of water mains to dwellings and efforts to improve railway services to Wellington and Stafford. The stationmaster during the 1920s was James Jones. Freddie Cooper, an employee of C & W Walker who lost an arm in an accident, manned the level crossing by the station and waved a red flag to stop motorists and pedestrians when a train was due. Freddie also acted as caretaker at the Primitive Methodist chapel.

The Coal Wharf itself was situated on the eastern corner of School Road and Wellington Road, alongside the branch railway which led from the main Wellington-Stafford line southwards to the Granville Colliery. Customers would fill their sacks and trolley them over the road to a weighing machine set into the ground on the corner of Wellington Road and Station Road, outside coal merchant George Hayward's house and office. In 1938, a hundredweight of coal cost about two shillings and was generally the only means by which homes could be heated and food cooked. There was another railway crossing with the customary white gates across the old Wellington-Newport main road adjacent to the Coal Wharf until the 1980s. In latter years, these were operated automatically and had flashing warning lights.

Other properties at the Coal Wharf included Freddie Martin's cycle shop, May Shepherd's billiards and snooker hall and the Co-operative Wholesale Society store managed by Mr Lowe. May Shepherd's nearby timber newspaper shop burned down around 1938 and was immediately rebuilt in brick (it was subsequently acquired by the Browns); behind it were two corrugated iron houses where the Shepherds lived.

The 1920s and 1930s also saw other small trading ventures in the area. Miss Pitts sold paraffin, Mrs Brown made toffee, Willy Morgan sold sweets, groceries and fireworks, Joe Clay had a smallholding (as did Jack Pearce who also ran The Sutherland Arms; when children came

The Coal Wharf section of Wellington Road, Donnington, mid-1930s, looking east. The Primitive Methodist chapel is on the right and the entrance to Station Road is on the left. The two children on the left are standing next to the weighbridge set into the road surface. Part of C & W Walker's Midland Iron Works can be seen, centre left.

Station Road, Donnington, c. 1930, looking north. The buildings on both sides of the road belonged to C & W Walker Ltd. The offices are to the right, an erecting shop to the left. Walker's internal railway track crosses the road at the bottom of the photograph.

Donnington Wood
CORONATION FESTIVITIES,
22nd JUNE, 1911.

The Children's Tea will be in the Dining Hall, Donnington, at 3-30 p.m. Each Child must please bring a mug, and every Chlid is requested to be on the Institute Recreation Ground not later than 2 p.m. The Meat Tea for Parishioners of sixty years and upwards, will be in the Dining Hall, at 4-30 p.m. The Committee regrets that it is absolutely impossible to provide knives and forks, and each person must please bring his or her own. It has been decided to give a Dinner in the Schools, at one o'clock, to all men who have contributed, or do contribute, not less than Ninepence to the Funds. It has also been decided to give a Meat Tea in the Dining Hall, at 4-30 p.m., to all women who have contributed, or do contribute, a similar amount. Both at the men's Dinner and the Women's Tea, persons must please bring their own knives and forks. No Tickets will be issued after Saturday, the 17th June. Sports will be held on the Institute Recreation Ground in the Afternoon and Evening, and the Committee has arranged for a Fine Display of Fireworks at dusk. Collectors will wait upon the various districts (which they have already visited) to supply Tickets and receive donations from those who have not already contributed.

WALTER PERRY,
Hon. Sec.

31st May, 1911.

Special occasions were the source of much merriment and provided a welcome relief from the constant struggles of everyday life. Celebrations to commemorate events involving Royalty were especially popular. The notice refers to the Mechanics Institute Recreation Ground, i.e. The Bell Fields. The Dining Room mentioned was inside C & W Walker's Midland Iron Works and hosted a wide variety of entertainment for many years.

for bottles of beer to take to their fathers working in the fields at harvest time, Jack sealed the tops with red sealing wax to prevent them from partaking en route). A small public house, set back from the road, operated about a hundred metres east of the post office.

With the sale of much of their local property before and during the First World War, the role played by the Leveson Gowers considerably reduced after almost 400 years of influence. Charles Walker and R.J. Milbourne (managing director of C & W Walker Ltd) gained the respect and support of local folk, who thereafter sought help from them in civic matters, where previously they would have approached the Duke.

The council concerned itself with matters of minor importance by present standards: stray horses from the pits causing a nuisance in 1913 (even as late as 1927, the Freehold Pit alone employed 36 horses, ponies and donkeys alongside its 314 colliers); the improvement of postal facilities; motor car warning notices (1922), white lines on the main road (1937) and council-controlled road repairs (even as late as 1943 the Lilleshall Company was responsible for the maintenance of its own 'unadopted' – non-public – roads). In 1918 the Lilleshall Company agreed to demolish sixty dilapidated houses, build sixty new ones and renovate fifty-three others.

Edward James, who owned Donnington Farm, was something of a philanthropist and paid for electric street lighting to be installed along Wellington Road in the early 1930s. Edward was a gentleman farmer, highly respected by his workers and local people. He also held an important position at Walcott Sugar Beet Factory. During the 1914 Lilleshall Estate sales he not only purchased the farm but also about eighteen cottages, including gamekeeper's and shepherd's dwellings near The Humbers, as accommodation for his employees. Furthermore, he paid for the erection of Lilleshall Memorial Hall in memory of his parents. Donnington Farm itself was managed by his bailiff, Elijah Millward. After his death in 1932, Edward's will stipulated that certain of the tenants were to continue living in their homes rent free until their own deaths.

Wellington Road, Donnington, c. 1910, looking west.

The ruins of Waxhill colliery buildings and nearby dwellings in the late 1920s. The Waxhill pits closed around 1905. Some of its colliers were able to find employment in the Freehold and Granville pits but the area fell into inevitable decline and dereliction. People continued to live in dreadful conditions at the Waxhills until the 1930s when many were rehoused in the newly-contructed Jubilee Avenue. Lilleshall Hill can be seen in the distance, centre right.

The ruins of the once magnificent Lodge Furnaces in the late 1920s. These furnaces were last used in 1888 and the structure allowed to decay after the Lilleshall Company shifted its mainstay operations to Snedshill and St Georges. The furnace towers were constructed from local Grinshill sandstone; during the 1960s, some of the stone was used for extensive alterations to St Matthew's church which had been built in 1845 using the same type of stone.

Both sides of a Smallholders Championship medal, probably dating from the early 1930s. It was discovered in a garden in what is now Baldwin Webb Avenue on the site of a former allotment.

It was not until the 1930s that Newport Rural District Council embarked on a programme of slum clearance which hitherto it had not been able to afford. The slums involved were the old barrack houses at Donnington Wood, Queens Road and Waxhill, together with those at Forge Row (now Smith's Crescent on the Cinder Hill) and Mechanics Row (in the corner of the junction of Oakengates Road and St Georges Road). Ten new houses were built in Jubilee Avenue but further local government reorganisation left the completion of the project to Wellington Rural District Council who subsequently erected another eighty-four houses. The avenue was named after King George V's Silver Jubilee in 1935. Reasonably-sized garden allotments were provided to encourage a degree of self-sufficiency in domestic food production.

The coal mining industry experienced further decline. At the beginning of the century there were several pits still working, notably the Waxhill, Muxtonbridge, Barn Pit, Freehold, Grange and Granville Collieries. Of these, the latter three were more productive. The Barn Pit shut down in 1902 and Waxhill closed around 1905, although its engine continued to pump water from the mines into the canal until abbout 1930. Muxtonbridge ceased production in 1912. The Freehold closed in 1928 owing to the high costs involved in pumping water out of the mine; 305 miners lost their jobs. It had always had a reputation for being the wettest pit in the coalfield; miners often had to work in waist-high freezing water.

Very little regard was shown for public safety after these mines ceased production; it was normal practice to leave the shafts exposed and simply encircle them with a minimal quantity of barbed wire wrapped around rusty metal posts. Locals then used them for tipping rubbish into. The same applied to older abandoned pits, including one on land behind the shops on Queens Road, which were only remedied if the ground was required for housing.

The turn of the century witnessed an increase in miners willing to embrace trade unionism but for many years they were obliged to do so covertly. Fearful that they could lose their jobs or be otherwise victimised by their employers should their union membership be discovered, members were given small tokens when their quarterly subscriptions were paid. The tokens, of varying shapes, were inscribed 'Salop Miners Federation' (an association had been formed in 1886) together with a letter or number allocated to the quarterly membership period. Tokens had two holes drilled into them so that they could be sewn underneath jacket lapels and thus be hidden from their employers. This practice continued until at least the late 1920s.

William Latham: Miners' Trade Union leader and Baptist lay preacher. He was regarded as something of a firebrand, leading the unsuccessful strike in 1913 for better pay and conditions for local colliers. Nevertheless, his persistence led to an improvement in local mining safety.

Some disillusionment in the power and protection supposedly offered by the union followed a strike called by the Salop Miners' secretary William Latham in 1913. The union was unable to provide finance for striking members whose families were forced to live off handouts from local churches. The strike collapsed. The General Strike of 1926 was something else entirely and showed the Government that ordinary people did have power to influence events even though the miners eventually had to admit defeat.

The brick kilns in Donnington Wood ceased production in the early years of the century and, apart from C & W Walker's and the mines, there were no large employers in the area. The once busy landscape deteriorated into an industrial wasteland. Mine and canal buildings fell into disrepair and dilapidation. The canal became overgrown with weeds and silted up; fishing there was no longer possible although some took advantage of fish in a pool which had appeared on the site of the former brick and tile works behind The Bell Inn.

Some colliers left the mines between 1910 and 1930 to start their own businesses; Harry Brown, for example, began a horse-drawn wagonette service to carry passengers to Oakengates market. Some people are still convinced two of his horses were called 'Damn' and 'Blast'. Eventually he bought several motorised omnibuses and expanded the service. In the 1940s, H. Brown & Sons Ltd began coach tour operations which enabled local folk to visit Manchester, other cities and seaside resorts. Other omnibus companies appeared during the 1920s, including Martlew's and Smith's, and provided similar services to a public keen to widen their horizons.

Rivalry in those early days was strong and even led to fist fights between competing drivers to decide which of them would take the queue of bemused passengers to Wellington or Oakengates. Before the Garrison terminus was created in the 1940s, people would congregate near The Shawbirch at Furnace Lane. This was no way to run a business so the various bus companies in the district formed a loose alliance called the Oakengates and District Small Bus Association which helped to resolve disagreements and devised a fairer way of allocating service runs between settlements.

The association introduced brass return tokens or tickets (paper ones had not yet been invented); each token was embossed with a unique number or letter assigned to one of the

Above left: Both sides of a Martlew's Coachways Return Fare ticket of a type first seen in the 1930s when the SOA agreed to incorporate a discount voucher valid in Dickins store at Oakengates.

Above centre: Brass Oakengates and District Small Bus Association Return ticket valid for journeys between Donnington and Oakengates and Donnington and Wellington. These tokens were used during the late 1920s and early 1930s before paper tickets were introduced. Each bus operator had his own supply of tokens embossed with his allocated number and gave one to each passenger on the outward journey. Passengers could use the token on any operator's bus for the return journey. A monthly 'reckoning' took place between the operators to balance their accounts.

Above right: Both sides of a Shropshire Omnibus Association Single Fare ticket of the type first issued in the 1930s. Advertising timetables (which frequently changed) was intended not only to increase service revenue but also to recoup printing costs.

A Martlew's service bus outside its garage at Queens Road, Donnington Wood, in the 1950s. Buses like this were supposed to seat about twenty-six passengers but were frequently packed with over sixty people together with bulging shopping bags as they crawled along the Wellington route on market days.

member companies. The idea behind the scheme was that a return ticket was given to each passenger travelling to, for example, Wellington. Because there was no guarantee the same company would be in service for the return journey, the ticket was handed to whichever company carried the passengers back home. A 'reckoning' was held at regular intervals and cash exchanged to balance each operator's books (although some operators were more reluctant to pay their share than others).

During the 1930s, after public bus services became subject to regulation, the association renamed itself the Shropshire Omnibus Association (SOA) and sought to regularise and rationalise their services in opposition to the Midland Red Omnibus Company. Local accountant Leonard Ross and later Bob Tranter acted as secretary and succeeded in protecting the interests of its members (even from each other). Paper tickets were introduced, some with money off vouchers to be used in certain shops in the area.

Competition between SOA members and the Midland Red frequently led to accusations of poaching, obstruction and unfair practice. For example, one Midland Red bus often loitered outside the old Swan Hotel at Wellington in order to pick up passengers on a connecting service from Dawley. The problem was that the bus obstructed the road, making it impossible for SOA buses to get past. Return tickets for SOA journeys were abandoned, then rapidly reinstated when the Midland Red itself introduced them.

The advent of motor transport also led to the arrival of haulage businesses: E. Hemmings & Son commenced trading in 1926. Their premises were acquired by McPhillips (Wellington) Ltd in 1974 after Hemmings moved outside the Donnington area. The land is now occupied by Tin Tin Cantonese Restaurant, Athena Vehicles and Townsend Croft. Several coal merchants (like Sid Bradley) were also able to expand their activities with the use of motor vehicles. In recent years, increased use of private cars has resulted in the advent of garages and petrol stations.

Earliest known photograph of the Donnington Wood Football Club, c. 1925. Before The Bell Fields became their home pitch, the team played on Billy Ormond's field south of the Black Bank. From left to right, back row: Wilf Wild, Sam Stamworth, Jim Gaut, Alf Plimmer, Eric Darn, George Dean, Billy Foulks, Jack Meredith. Front row: Billy Hayward, Bill Rigby, Jack Mainwaring, Percy Hicks, Johnny Hayward, Jim Lane.

The Miners' Welfare Fund financed the purchase of the public recreation ground at School Road, which then consisted of a bowling green, two tennis courts, pavilion, football and cricket pitches (when cattle and sheep were not grazing). The land was acquired in December 1925 from the Duke of Sutherland and the first trustees of the grounds were Thomas Bould, Thomas Leese, Thomas William Wallace, Albert Enos Hayward, Samuel Colley, Enos Richard Lowe, Walter Perry, William Pickering and Thomas Leonard Bott, all of whom had close ties with or lived in Donnington Wood. The grounds, as well as nearby spoil heaps, were used for covert gambling by colliers; 3- and 5-card brag and spinning Put-and-Take dice games were especially popular. Gamblers' children often acted as police lookouts.

The Bell Inn was the centre of much musical and sporting activity for many years during the nineteenth and twentieth centuries. Its success must have been due to continued hospitality and support given by its landlords, particularly Jim Lees, Charlie Chadfield, Archie Side, Stan Oliver and, during the 1950s and 1960s, Alf Whittingham. Since 2000 it has been run by Dean and Julie Boulton and renamed Joeys, the name of Julie's father.

In 1902, William Lawrence, a talented euphonium and violin player already with an excellent reputation, offered his services and the Donnington Wood Institute Band was resurrected. He became bandmaster and in September 1904 the band won the Quickstep contest at St Georges Wakes. They entered more competitions during the next few years, achieving several placings but never a first. In 1907 the band was catastrophically unplaced in a competition at Shrewsbury which led to William Lawrence appealing to his band to 'think musically'. They did. In June 1908 they won the County Championship and arrived home very late. The people of Donnington Wood were woken up by the band playing 'See the conquering hero comes!' as they strolled along the dark lanes back to The Bell.

The band went on to win more competitions, including the County Championship an unprecedented four times in succession. St Georges Temperance Band made an official objection to the result of the 1910 competition but their appeal was rejected; in an act of mischievous jubilation, the Donnington Wood Band gave an impromptu performance at the

The Donnington Wood Institute Band, celebrating their deserved success at the Shrewsbury competition in 1908. They are in the grounds of the National School with St Matthew's church in the background. Bandmaster William Lawrence is seated at the front holding his pet dog behind the coveted trophy. Jim Lees, landlord of The Bell Inn and a reliable supporter of all things sporting and cultural, is standing on the extreme left.

crossroads in St Georges, rubbing salt into a very open wound. The rivalry between the (by that time) three St Georges bands and the Donnington Wood Brass Band continued for several years.

The outbreak of the First World War brought an end to the Donnington Wood Brass Band. Many of its members perished during the war. The band was revived for a short time in 1924, again under the leadership of William Lawrence. He died in December that year and was buried in St Matthew's churchyard. The band played him out.

William's son, also named William, took up the reins of office but, despite another ten years or so of public appearances, things were never the same and the band eventually ceased to function. A last attempt to resurrect failing fortunes occurred during the 1940s under the leadership of Tom Dodd, without success.

The Donnington Wood Institute Male Voice Society (later the Donnington Wood & District Male Voice Society) was formed in 1922 and also based at The Bell Inn. The first conductor was Jim Ferriday and early members were Dick Parker, Jabe Lake, Les Brothwood, Fred Wakely and Percy Hicks. Walter Hobson became conductor (as well as choirmaster at St Matthew's church) in 1928, when Jim left the area, and continued in this role until his death, aged ninety-one. The choir won many contests, including the Midlands Championship in 1948, and regularly broadcast on BBC radio from 1939.

The Donnington Wood Institute Male Voice Society, c. 1928, with two of their trophies. Walter Hobson sits centre front holding his baton. The choir, many of whose members also sang in the Sankey Male Voice Choir, is pictured outside the Mechanics Institute near The Bell Inn; already in a ramshackle state, the building only lasted a few more years before it was demolished.

Members of the Gymnastics Club which met at the United Methodist chapel in School Road during the 1920s.

The ladies section of the Donnington Wood Tennis Club, c. 1935. They met at the Miners' Welfare grounds near The Bell Inn. From left to right: Nellie Withington, Margaret Cooper, Lydia Onions, Myrtle Rigby, Gladys Barber, Bernice Owen. Coincidentally, all, except Myrtle, were schoolteachers.

Ten

After 1939

By far the greatest impact on Donnington and Muxton was the re-siting of the War Department's Central Ordnance Depot (COD) of Woolwich Arsenal at Donnington on land to the north of the old Wellington-Newport road. The influence of local government began to increase with the national government's decision to move the Woolwich Arsenal to a safer place in preparation for the impending Second World War. Donnington was chosen; the land, being in close proximity to the Weald Moors, was prone to fog and mist and the local council was receptive to War Ministry proposals.

The creation of what was, in effect, a new town to accommodate both army and civilian personnel undoubtedly reversed social and economic decline in the area. At the same time it heralded the disappearance of vast tracts of farmland. The 450 acres occupied by the COD alone comprised about half of the land farmed by Edward James at Donnington Farm; that belonging to Donnington Wood Farm was almost completely covered by the housing estate. Most locals refer to the COD as The Depot or, less affectionately, The Dump.

In the years leading up to the Second World War, following representations made by Col. James Baldwin Webb, MP for the Wrekin, Wellington Rural District Council agreed to a proposal to site the establishment and be responsible for the development of 'New Donnington', an enormous council housing estate formally opened by the Minister of Health, Rt Hon Ernest Brown, in 1943. Many workers at the COD arrived before their families and were billeted on local people, even as far away as Wellington, until homes had been built for them.

During the war, the COD saw some 15,000 soldiers garrisoned in its grounds and was responsible for the storage and despatch of all manner of supplies to operational personnel scattered around areas of conflict throughout the world. Service and repair of military equipment was also carried out. The centre, now with a much diminished workforce and negligible military presence, continues its essential service; in recent years it has provided support for the Falklands, Gulf and Balkan conflicts and various other NATO operations. For reasons of national security, it was not until the 1960s that Ordnance Survey maps showed any evidence of the depot's existence.

The military authorities commandeered other plots of land for various purposes. While the COD was being built, army engineers were billeted in the school room behind the Primitive Methodist chapel at the Coal Wharf, even though it only had one toilet. Other soldiers had barracks on land (next to the Sutherland Arms) which became The Willows Caravan Park for residential caravans during the 1960s, now called Breton Park Residential Park Homes. Eventually several wooden huts were erected for army personnel, displaced persons and prisoners of war in other parts of Donnington, like the playing fields around the Little Theatre on Wellington Road. Army vehicles were parked on land now occupied by part of Coronation Drive.

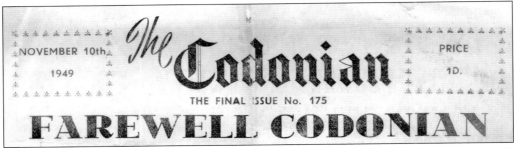

NOVEMBER 10th 1949

The **Codonian**

THE FINAL ISSUE No. 175

PRICE 1D.

FAREWELL CODONIAN

Masthead of the final issue of The Codonian, *the fortnightly internal newspaper of COD Donnington personnel. During its 175 issues it made an invaluable contribution to settling the imported workforce into its new locality and provided an extensive range of news, entertainment and sporting coverage.*

Construction of just one of the many storage buildings at COD Donnington, c. 1940. Many men were employed on this major undertaking. Building contractors included Henry Boot & Sons, Tarmac Ltd, Colston Electrical Company and Hayden's. Their workers were billeted in Shrewsbury, Wellington and Wolverhampton, as well as in the immediate locality, and travelled daily by bus to Donnington.

New Donnington incorporated a massive council housing estate of over 800 dwellings and 12 shops in the area bounded by Furnace Lane, Park Road, Queens Road, School Road and the main road from the Coal Wharf back to Furnace Lane. Owing to a severe timber shortage, many of the buildings have flat roofs, some of which have since been crowned with shallow-angle apex roofs. Some of the new streets were named after local councillors (such as Hayward Avenue) and the Member of Parliament, Baldwin Webb Avenue. (Baldwin Webb died along with about 500 children being evacuated to Canada at the start of the war. The ship they were on sank in the Atlantic Ocean and everyone on board perished.) Similar criteria have been exercised in subsequent development (as in Cordingley Way) but fortunately some historical associations have not been overlooked; Meadow Road, Waxhill and Barn Closes are all named after local coal pits, Farm Lane (called Alder Lane in 1813) after Donnington Wood Farm.

An air-raid shelter was built for civilian use in the corner of School Road and The Fields; it was demolished in 1948. Householders were issued with gas masks and Anderson Shelters. Fortunately, there was only one air raid during the hostilities, when bombs fell harmlessly into nearby woods. C & W Walker Ltd ran their own Home Guard Platoon to fill the gaps in defence left by the professional army. The Platoon was disbanded after the victory celebrations but civilian fighting spirit continued to be fostered by the Territorial Army at the Drill Hall near the Shawbirch Inn.

After 1945, vast quantities of damaged, obsolete or simply surplus equipment, including radios and binoculars and even lorries and tilly vans, were taken away by the lorry load and, under the watchful eye of armed sentries, cast into disused mines. Memories are divided about which pits were used; the Freehold is the main contender but Waxhill and Lodge Bank mines are also mentioned. Whichever mines were used, they were afterwards filled with tons of rubble to make it impossible for items to be recovered.

Donnington Farm provided temporary accommodation for army officers and batmen; it was acquired by Whitbread Brewery around 1940 and became the White House Hotel, acting as a 'Honeymoon Hotel' for soldiers getting married and having limited leave in which to celebrate their nuptials. Remaining land, belonging to the farm, was acquired by the Ward family who farmed at Lubstree. Occasionally local residents accommodated prospective brides and their relatives as there were no recognised lodging houses in the area. There used to be a tennis court where the car park to the White House Hotel now stands. The hotel was later acquired by Ansells Brewery. James Swindley became licensee almost forty years ago and purchased the business from the brewery in the early 1980s.

Shopping centres were built at The Parade, Albert Place and in Queens Road to cater for a rapidly growing population; existing shops in Donnington and Donnington Wood continued to function for many years although the majority, like the butcher's at the Bell Corner, have now disappeared. The Bell Stores, once run by Frank Nelson, has managed to survive. Wally the barber and Jack Smith's betting shop had premises at the Coal Wharf during and after the war. The Co-op store there closed down around 1960 in deference to the newer, larger premises at The Parade.

New post offices were opened inside the COD (where the business was called Codonia) and at The Parade. The post office in Wellington Road, Donnington, originated many years

Following two pages: *Ordnance Survey map revised 1948-49 showing the extent of the New Donnington housing development in relation to the surrounding area. In the interests of national security, the COD Donnington site is not shown and would continue to be omitted from maps until the 1960s. The names of a few disused pits are shown, although the former Freehold Colliery (on the hill west of Muxtonbridge Colliery) has been omitted. Much of Donnington Wood south of the course of the former canal was, at this time, still in a state of decay and dereliction. Muxton continued to be little more than a 'ribbon' village limited to either side of Muxton Lane. The present Field House Drive preserves the name of Field House, situated close to the former mineral railway.*

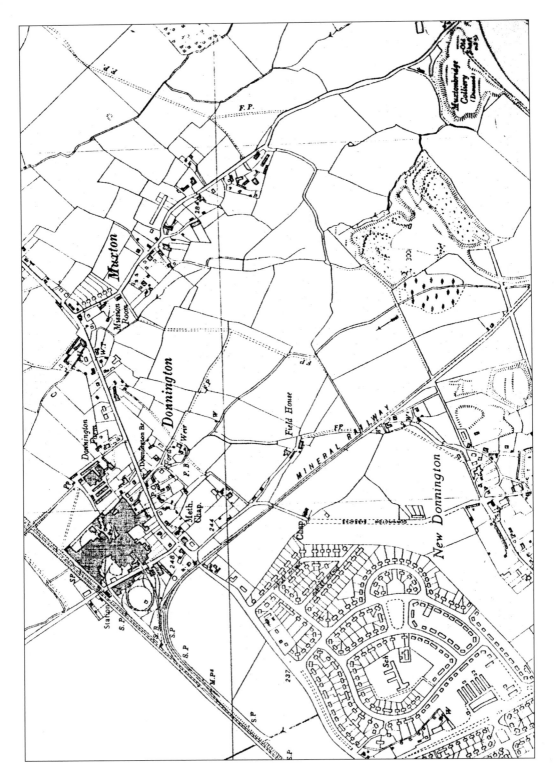

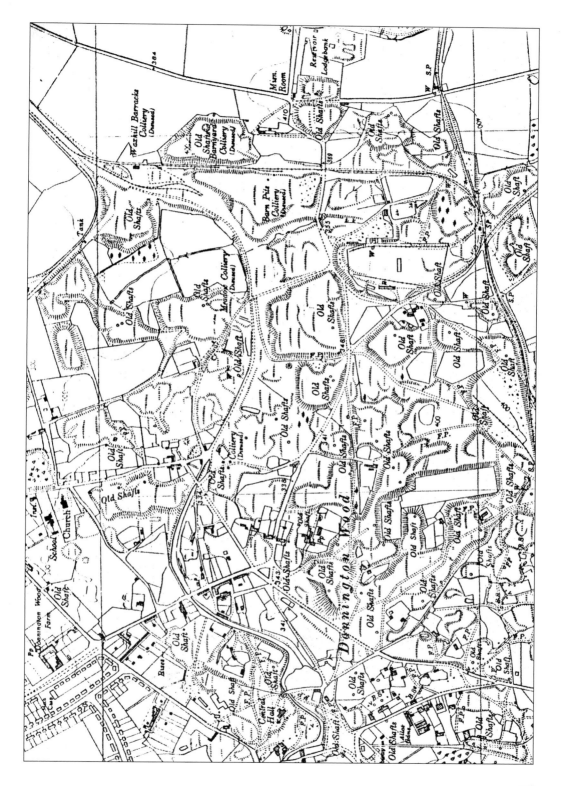

85

Postmaster Ernest Thorpe outside the former wooden Muxton post office at Donnington in the early 1980s.

before and had been run during the 1920s by James Vandrill and, after his death, his wife before moving to a room in Walter Hobson's house where it was operated by Walter's wife Emily, Mrs Vandrill's daughter. Ernest Thorpe was appointed sub-postmaster in December 1940 and ran the business from the front room of his house adjacent to C & W Walker's, where he was also employed. In 1946, Ernest bought a small wooden grocery shop from Miss Annie Owen on the opposite side of the road and subsequently moved the post office into it. At some time, possibly during the 1980s, the post office designated itself as at Muxton to reduce confusion between it and the office on The Parade, even though it was situated in Donnington itself. The business was transferred into Ernest's daughter's name – Rozanne Lembicz – in 1986 when the building was renovated into the present brick-built, more secure, premises.

By 1979 the COD had a token army complement but provided work for over 4,000 civilians, and was (indeed still is, even with a much depleted workforce) of great economic importance to Donnington. The COD changed its name during the late 1980s to BOD (Base Ordnance Depot) and is now called the DSDC (Donnington Storage and Distribution Centre). In September 1983 and April 1988 it suffered two devastating fires when a combined total of well over £350 million worth of damage was caused. Public health fears from asbestos fall-out led to intensive council clean-up operations covering an area well over five miles to the north and west of the depot.

New Donnington was designed by the architect J. Brian Cooper. Several plots of land were left undeveloped for the future building of churches and recreational facilities. Turreff Hall, for example, was built by the American Army (who used Donnington as a transit camp) who intended laying a bowling green and tennis courts on the adjoining land. This failed to materialise (the war ended). The premises were used by a women's club during the war. The public library and Champion Jockey public house were built there during the 1960s; the Turreff Hall was home to a youth club at that time. The Hall is named after Revd Albert Turreff, chairman of Wellington Rural District Council when New Donnington was being planned. The police station on Wellington Road and police houses at the Four Ways were also built then; the station has been unmanned for several years (although still used for police

ROBINSON CRUSOE

| Producer | ... | ... | ... | BILLIE CARTER |
| Co-Producer ... | ... | ... | MICHAEL OLIVER |

CAST

Robinson Crusoe	EILEEN COX
Sam Snorer (*his sleeping partner*)	CLIFFORD WILSON
Bob Down (*a planter*)...	HARRY MASON
Ma Fiddler (*a local trader*)	AUBREY WARD
Maria } (*Brazilian dancing girls*) {	MARIE LATHAM
Pepita	MAVIS WEBB
Captain Cummango (*of the sailing ship El Codonia*)	WALTER GIBLETT
Amanda (*his daughter*)	EVE SLINGER
Don Ramon Lupez Hernando De Soto (*a " playboy "*)	PETER HOSKYNS
Jack Ahoy (*a sailor*)	RAY HARLAND
Man Friday	BOBBY GRATTIDGE
Mulligatawny (*the cannibal king*)	MICHAEL OLIVER
Kedgeree (*the cannibal queen*)	SHELAGH MCMASTER
Captain Crossbones (*the pirate captain*)	FRANK TURK
Johnny Windup (*his mate*)	ALAN COX
Wall-Eye Willy (*his mate*)	ALAN GLEW

Dancers: John Payne, Roy Harland and " The Carbray Lovelies," Gaynor Higgs, Anne Honeywell, Rita Gratten, Betty Dawes, Brenda Broad, Barbara Mullis, Sheila Buck.

Chorus—Ladies: Zena Enticknap, Maureen Eastwell, Pam Davies, Muriel Giblett, Doreen Stewart, Ann Jones, Vera Elias, Sally Gittens.
Gentlemen: Ray Thorniwill, Mick Guy, Dennis Chadwick, Donald Wildblood, John Payne, Alan Cox, Frank Turk, Alan Glew, John Travers, Ken March.

Cast list of Robinson Crusoe, *the first production performed in the Little Theatre, 1953.*

The cast of the 1961 Humpty Dumpty pantomime production. The Donnington Garrison Amateur Dramatic and Operatic Society have staged several pantomimes over the years. During the 1950s and 1960s, amateur productions such as this were popular crowd-pullers and, even allowing for stage fright, fluffed lines and props that behaved contrary to expectations, were always met with genuine appreciation and enthusiasm.

accommodation) and is currently scheduled for rebuilding.

Other vacant land was intended for the building of a new Anglican church and vicarage (hence the name Church Walk). This plan was scrapped and instead a residential home for the elderly built on the site. It was felt that St Matthew's church was sufficiently near to the new centre of population and the building of another church could not be justified, although the road retains its name. Donnington Wood Farm became a fire station in 1940 and later housed an ambulance station until the late 1970s when a health centre was built on the site.

Musical entertainment continued in different guises during and after the Second World War. During the bleak war years, concerts, dances, 'gang' shows, pantomimes, plays and other musical entertainment took place in the dining room at C & W Walker's (on the opposite side of Station Road from the main works; it provided seating for up to 500 people), the Coddon Club, the Church Institute, the Officers' Mess at Parson's Barracks and at the newly built Garrison Theatre (later renamed the Globe Theatre which has since followed the well trodden path of many cinemas nationally, now offering the attractions of bingo) where films were also shown.

The Eric Jacobs Trio was formed with Eric Jacobs on violin, William Lawrence (grandson of the first bandmaster of Donnington Wood Brass Band and son of the second) playing piano and Enoch Fenn on double bass. The trio were extremely talented and very well received at performances held locally as well as in venues outside the area. The Community Centre by The Globe opened in 1975.

The origins of The Little Theatre are to be found during this period when entertainment was a particularly important aspect of keeping up public morale. Although Brigadier de Woolf inaugurated the Orpheus Society, two people were to prove essential in the establishment of entertainment groups such as The Estateers and, in 1951, the Donnington

Garrison Amateur Dramatic and Operatic Society: Stan and Billie Carter, who continued as true stalwarts until their retirement in 1965. The first production of the society took place in 1952 and, after five other shows, moved into its present premises, a former indoor rifle range, in 1953. It opened with a performance of *Robinson Crusoe* and has since gained an excellent reputation for its many and varied productions. Incidentally, Peter Dakin, who appeared as a minstrel in the 1964 revue *Cavalcade of Song*, went on to appear in *The Black and White Minstrel Show* on BBC Television. Suspected arson gutted the stage area in a fire in September 1978 which took almost six months to refurbish. Further improvements to facilities have been ongoing. In 1987 the society renamed itself The Little Theatre Donnington Society when the Army could no longer fund its activities; the premises were acquired by the Wrekin District Council and the society now rents the building from the Telford and Wrekin Council.

The COD catered extremely well for its transplanted workforce and the people of New Donnington. It appears that integration with the indigenous populations at Muxton, Donnington and Donnington Wood was incredibly easy, unlike the initial reaction to migrants from the Birmingham area who moved into south Telford in the 1970s. Perhaps the locals felt some sympathy towards so many families being resettled at so critical a time in British history. Furthermore, the COD provided work for many local folk who worked alongside and formed close relationships with the newcomers.

The COD not only provided employment; it also provided the Army Ordnance Services Canteen and, in 1942, the Coddon ('COD DON'nington) social club buildings and a fortnightly newspaper, *The Codonian*, for its personnel. The newspaper was packed with information explaining the historical aspects of Shropshire, local news and entertainment

Members of the Donnington Garrison Amateur Dramatic and Operatic Society during the early 1960s. The society has consistently provided excellent performances of a wide variety of theatrical, dramatic and musical productions; its Gilbert and Sullivan operettas have always been particularly well received by appreciative audiences.

and many sporting features, all of which helped to settle people into their new environment. The last issue was published in November 1949. The Coddon became a focal point for sport and boasted its own cycling, cricket, football, bowls, billiards, snooker, darts, dominoes, etc., clubs, not in competition with but rather in addition to the sporting clubs already in existence around The Bell Inn and surrounding townships.

The Miners' Welfare grounds near The Bell Inn also witnessed an upsurge in sporting developments; tennis courts were built in 1948 and the tennis club, apparently established during the 1930s, now consisted of sixty-five adult and nine junior members (paying subscriptions of 10s and 5s per week respectively during the season). Among those playing regularly on the grey shale courts from the early days were Cecil Herring, Don Johnson, Ivy Lingard, Frank and Bessie Mansell, Jean Martin, Barbara Molineux, Ken Mullinder, George and Myrtle Rigby, Frank Spencer and George and Nellie Withington. The club shared an old wooden pavillion with the bowling and football clubs.

The recreation grounds were acquired in 1956, despite some local opposition, by the Wellington Rural District Council who subsequently built two additional tarmacadam tennis courts, a new pavillion, swimming and paddling pools. They also permitted the playing of matches on Sundays, something previously forbidden under the terms of the original Miner's Welfare Trusteeship. The tennis club disbanded around 1969. The recreation ground now seems very neglected and run down. Nevertheless, the site constitutes a public amenity; hopefully the present council will not let it be used for yet more building development.

The Donnington Wood Football Club continued to perform well after the war and won many trophies in various leagues, although it also managed to maintain a reputation for hard play; referees as well as players had to be carried off on occasion. One noteworthy match in the 1950s was against Newtown in the final of the Welsh Amateur Cup; after much fouling and fighting between players and spectators, the match had to be abandoned. Donnington Swifts junior football team, set up by Harold Emery, Jack Harrison and Bill Mears, played between 1954 and 1962.

Members of the CODDON Cricket Club, c. 1950.

90

Members of the bowls and tennis sections of the CODDON Sports and Social Club, with their trophies, c. 1949. From left to right: -?-, -?-, -?-, Jim Thorpe, Irene Oxford (née Pitchford), Peter Phillips, Marion Phillips (holding two trophies), Joe Leeke, Lillian Leeke, Mr Watkins, Jim Bradley and Ernie Oxford.

The war years also brought rationing. Residents had to be registered with shops in order to obtain their quota of basic foodstuffs such as bread, butter and meat as well as clothing, petrol and coal. George Hayward at the Coal Wharf often let people fill their sacks with slack for virtually nothing when their coal ration had been used up. The Shropshire Omnibus Association was forced to reduce its services for a while; bus owners tried to object but were told their ration books would be withdrawn if they used more petrol than they were allowed. However, demand for services increased as workers, contractors and army personnel needed to be transported daily to the COD. As a result, green corrugated iron bus shelters were erected on land now occupied by Aldi supermarket.

Despite the harsh regime imposed by rationing, farmers frequently supplied additional eggs and milk to their regular customers and friends. Much black marketeering took place and American soldiers based in Donnington were extremely popular with their seemingly never-ending supplies of nylon stockings and chocolate. Messrs Rushton and Hitchin did the rounds killing and preparing domestic pigs as they had done before the outbreak of war. Pigkeeping continued in older parts of Donnington until the 1950s; it was said every part of a pig could be used – except the squeal!

Nationalisation of the mines in 1947 forced the Lilleshall Company to sever its colliery connections in Donnington Wood. Both the Grange and Granville mines were extensively modernised immediately afterwards by the National Coal Board (NCB). The Grange Pit ceased operations as a single unit in 1952 and was latterly used to drain excess water from, and to provide a down draught for air circulation in, the Granville mine as well as an alternative exit route; it no longer extracted coal.

Colliers at the Granville mine went on strike with those in the rest of the country for higher pay and better working conditions in 1973 and were visited by Jo Gormley, leader of the Miners' Union. The ensuing Wilberforce enquiry upheld their claims and they won their

DONNINGTON WOOD
FOOTBALL CLUB

President: Chairman: Vice-Chairman
C. LAKE, Esq.   H. TANTER, Esq.   A. PALIN, Esq.

Treasurer — F. MARSH

Hon. Secretary — W. TRANTER
120, School Road, Donnington Wood, Shropshire.

Annual Dinner

FOREST GLEN PAVILION,
WREKIN, WELLINGTON.
SATURDAY. 11th JUNE, 1966
at 7.15 p.m.

Season 1949-50
Winners ... Shrewsbury Amateur Cup
Winners ..   Wellington League Cup
Champions ... ... Wellington League

1950-51
Winners ... County League Ch. Cup

1951-52
Winners   ... ... County League
Winners ... ... Clee Hill Cup

1952-53
Winners   ... ... County League
Winners ... ... Shropshire Junior Cup

1953-54
Winners   ... ... County League
Winners ... ... Clee Hill Cup

1954-55
Winners ... ... Clee Hill Cup

1955-56
Winners ... Shrewsbury Directors Cup

1956-57
Winners ... Bridgnorth Infirmary Cup

1957-58
Winners   ... ... County League
Winners ... Bridgnorth Infirmary Cup

1958-59
Winners ... Wolverhampton Ch. Cup
Winners ... . J. W. Hunt Cup

1959-60
Winners ... ... Shropshire Junior Cup
Winners ... Shrewsbury Directors Cup

1960-61
Winners   ... ... County League

1961-62
Winners ... Shrewsbury Amateur Cup

1962-63
Winners ... ... Shropshire Junior Cup
Winners ... Shrewsbury Amateur Cup

1963-64
Winners ... ... Welsh Amateur Cup
Winners ... County League Ch. Cup
Winners   ... ... County League

1964-65
Winners .. .. County Cup
Winners ... ... County League

Programme for the Donnington Wood Football Club Annual Dinner held at The Forest Glen, 1966. The programme proudly details some of the club's achievements.

case. However, increased wages and higher running costs soon took their toll. NCB operations in Donnington Wood were wound down as the mines were considered to be no longer economically viable; the Granville closed in 1979; new jobs at collieries outside Shropshire were found for some of the workforce. Donnington Wood's oldest industry, with the exception of farming, ceased to exist. The Grange Colliery pithead area is now occupied by a naturists' club and the Granville is a waste disposal site.

By 1951 the population had risen to 6,696, and has continued to rise with further housing development. As part of the Government's post-war slum clearance and rehousing project, prefabricated concrete-panelled dwellings were erected from 1953 in Coronation Drive (named after Queen Elizabeth's accession to the throne and intended to house miners transferred from the Durham Coalfield), Jubilee Avenue, Hayward Avenue, Queens Road and School Road. Some of the land had been used as vegetable allotments since before the war.

The structure of these particular properties gave rise to considerable concern during the 1980s when many tenants took advantage of the Conservative Government's policy which enabled them to purchase their own homes at greatly reduced cost. Unfortunately, because of structural faults, the council was obliged to repurchase many and carry out remedial and cosmetic work. Further low cost council housing was built on derelict mining land and the Old Yard to the south of The Common in the late 1960s. Many more private estates and business premises, including the council depot in St Georges Road, have been created on former farming and mining land, some of which has been rendered virtually sterile and even toxic by centuries of industrial exploitation. Responsibility for council housing passed to the Wrekin Housing Trust in 1999.

One of the steam engines used by the National Coal Board to transport coal extracted from the Granville Colliery, seen here in the mid-1950s. The engine hauled wagons along the mineral railway to link up with the Britsh Railway line near Walker's Works.

In many respects the service provided by local buses was similar to that given by railways a century earlier. It is difficult to appreciate how popular and heavily used these bus services were. During the 1940s to 1960s, the SOA ran services between Wellington, Donnington and Oakengates every five minutes throughout the day on Saturdays and virtually every bus would be packed full (even as many as sixty-five passengers on a twenty-six-seater bus!) for shopping and entertainment trips. Buses were, in effect, the lifeblood of society and provided a vital service for the benefit of businesses and the public. Even shorter and less populous routes were catered for; the SOA served almost every community scattered around the district.

There was continual acrimony between SOA members and their rivals, the Birmingham Midland Motor Omnibus Company (the 'Midland Red'), both sides accusing each other of picking passengers up at unauthorised points, 'lying in wait' at the bus terminuses in Wellington and Oakengates in an effort to poach passengers, poor timekeeping, overloading and operating on routes not approved by the Regional Traffic Commissioners at Birmingham.

In fact, such was the dog-eat-dog relationship between SOA members that they regularly accused each other of similar malpractice. Surprisingly, it was not until the late 1940s that recognised bus stops were introduced with Police and County Council Surveyor's approval; until then, buses could stop wherever passengers flagged them down.

Increasing use of private cars from the 1970s onwards has, for the time being at least, made bus transport unattractive except for those who have no choice but to make use of comparatively infrequent and often inconvenient services. In 1978, when the National Bus Company (trading locally under the name 'Tellus'), took over all services in the district, Brown's, Smith's and Martlew's amalgamated to form Britannia International Travel, which operates tours to various parts of Britain and the Continent as well as providing contract hire for schools and businesses. The current incarnation of bus services in Telford is operated under the trading name 'Arriva'.

Several garages, for example Don Service Station (now Van Beek's Motor Factors), and petrol stations were built along Wellington Road during the 1950s and 1960s (one, to the west of Jubilee Avenue, was on land occupied by the Cartwheel Café owned by Jack Cotton between around 1940 and 1960; two houses had previously stood there. The Cartwheel Café may have been previously called The Windmill Café, although a few residents seem to recall a café of that name near Brookside in the late 1940s and early 1950s.) Some garages have changed owners, others have closed down because of too much local competition and new ones have been built as a result of redesigned road systems. Wellington Road, once a main thoroughfare, has now become something of a backwater regarded as somewhat unsafe by motorists who feel the euphemistically named 'calming measures' are ill conceived and porrly designed.

The present population finds employment not only in the concerns already mentioned but also in innumerable new and old established industries of the Telford conurbation; an increasing number are employed in the tertiary (service) sector of the local economy.

Local government was revised in 1974 when the newly-formed Wrekin District Council absorbed five of the previous urban and rural districts.

In 1963 the Dawley Development Corporation was created to plan the expansion of Dawley into a new town. Government re-thinking led to the planning of a much larger new town stretching from Muxton to Ironbridge, and was named after the county's most famous

Opposite: *Entries extracted from* The Wrekin Civic and Commercial Directory, 1958. *The details cannot be regarded as a fully comprehensive listing of all businesses at that time; some were not willing to pay for their names to be mentioned. Furthermore, not all the entries are accurate; for example, the Donnington Wood Silver Prize band is mentioned even though it had effectively disbanded many years before.*

PUBLIC FACILITIES

Council Housing Manager
F Butterick, Estate Office, New Donnington
County Councillor
C F Cordingley, New Donnington
Councillors, Donnington Wood Ward
L Bullock, Field View, Wellington Road
Mrs G Cordingley, 53 Turreff Avenue
G Hayward, Baldwin Webb Avenue
G E Whyle, 84 School Road
Clinics, Doctors, Dentist
Ante-Natal & Child Welfare Centre, Turreff Hall.
Child Welfare Centre, Ordnance Depot
Dr W G Liggett. Residence: Wellington Road
Dr M I McEnroy, 1 Winifred's Drive
J M Pattison, 11 Wellington Road
A H Rennie, Wellington Road
Cultural Societies, etc.
Business & Professional Women's Club, secretary Mrs J B Yeo, 62 James Way
CODDON Club, R.O.A.C. Depot
Donnington Wood Amateur Football Club (& Bowling Club), Bell Ground (also Tennis Courts)
Donnington Wood Male Voice Choir
Donnington Wood Silver Prize Band, Bell Inn
Donnington Wood Recreation Ground
Donnington Wood St Matthew's Youth Club, Rev H R Jervis, The Vicarage, Wellington Road
Library, New Donnington
Turreff Hall, Turreff Avenue
Licensed Premises
Old Bell, Donnington Wood
Sutherland Arms, Wellington Road, Donnington
Post Offices
Donnington and Donnington (Wellington Road)
Schools
Donnington Wood C.E.
Donnington Wood County Infants

TRADES

Agricultural & Corn Merchants & Millers
Charles Morris, Brookside, Donnington (& Hay & Straw)
Donnington Wood Mill Co. Ltd
Coal Merchant
Syd Bradley, Donnington Wood
Chemist
E Margerrison, The Parade (& Wines & Spirits)
Cinema and Theatre
Garrison (Globe Cinema), Wellington Road
The Little Theatre, Wellington Road
Cycle & Motor Cycle Dealers
J F Martin, Wellington Road (& Electrical supplies, Radios & Televisions)

Confectioners, Food Suppliers and Caterers
Bell Corner Stores (W L Jones)
Jack Boyle, The Parade (& Florists)
Cartwheel Cafe, Wellington Road
H B Gallier, butcher, 10 The Parade
M E Gillam, Wrekin Drive (Florist & Seedsman)
G C Martin, Wellington Road (& Tobacconist)
H W Mason & Son, Queens Road
Oakengates Co-operative Society (Wellington Road, Farm Lane & mobile)
Phillips Stores Limited, The Parade
Queens Road Stores (Ashley's), New Estate, Donnington Wood (& General Stores)
B Richards Ltd, The Parade (& Hairdressers)
Smith's Bakery, The Parade
Thorpe's, Wellington Road (& Post Office)
Transport Cafe, Wellington Road
Decorators, Painters, Plumbers, Ironmongers
Frank Arnold, Landor, Wellington Road
S J Williams (Williams Bros), 11 The Parade (& Fishing Tackle)
Dry Cleaners & Launderers
Belle Vue Cleaners Ltd, 3 The Parade
Fancy Goods, General Stores &Hardware
L Brothwood, 12 The Parade (& Tobacconist)
Fish & Chip Shops
Brown's, Ivy House, Wellington Road
Jones', School Road
Garages, Haulage Contractors
E Hemmings & Son, Don Garage, Wellington Road (& Car Hire)
Horace W Rowley, 58 Wellington Road
Motor Coaches
Brown & Sons, Queens Road
Martlew's (Ashley Bros), Queens Road
W Smith & Son, 232 St Georges Road
Newsagents
N Pewdley, The Kiosk, South Gate, COD
Fred Spiers, 2 The Parade (& Tobacconist)
Nurserymen & Seedsmen
The Chestnuts Market Gardens (Vallings & Son), School Road
Yew Tree Market Gardens (Katenka & Son), Donnington Wood
Yew Tree Nursery (R L Millington), near Bell Inn (Bedding Plants, Wreathes, etc.)
Photographer
H G Bushby, School Road (Coal Wharf end)
Sectional Steel Structure Buildings, etc.
West Midlands Welded Structures Ltd, near Bell Inn, Donnington Wood
Wools, Knitwear & Art Needlework
Isabel Bryant, Ivy House, 10 Wellington Road
Mrs H Minor, 1 Wellington Road

civil engineer – Thomas Telford; thus the Telford Development Corporation came into existence.

When its work was virtually completed, full control of Telford's administration was handed over to the Wrekin District Council, which, under its present guise of Telford and Wrekin Council, covers an area slightly larger than the new town.

Both the council and the corporation have been responsible for many civic improvements in the Donnington area in recent years; sadly they are equally responsible for denuding the township of buildings and land representative of its industrial past. Public meetings were held during the early 1980s to determine what should happen to the extensive areas covered by pit mounds in Donnington Wood. Most people wanted the land to be left as it was, preserved as a monument to the past and somewhere in which they could walk; the majority didn't want estates of private housing, a golf course, a rubbish tip or business parks.

To the great annoyance of older residents, the council was instrumental in providing estates of private housing, a golf course, a rubbish tip and business parks, including the Donnington Campus Rejuvenation Project near the Old Lodge furnaces, currently under construction. This latest development of yet more business premises on levelled pit mounds makes it extremely difficult to carry out further archaeological investigations of earlier industrial activity buried beneath the spoil. It also encroaches further into open land and reduces the amount of ground available for leisure pursuits. Part of this development has been named the Stag Business Park, presumably because of its Medieval Deer Park origins.

In recent years, Donnington has lost several noteworthy buildings which have been rebuilt at the favoured Blists Hill museum rather than in close proximity to their historic origins. The Granville Country Park, now reduced in size but with a few former industrial sites remaining, is practically all that survives from the past.

Many pit mounds have disappeared during the last twenty years, including the Nobby Bank which once stood imposingly alongside St Georges Road on land partly occupied by ASDA supermarket since 2000. Older residents hope that a few of the pit mounds, mine workings and old buildings will be allowed to remain, a silent testimony to Donnington Wood's past.

There is no doubt that the Donnington area has developed a character of its own which reflects the old and new influences that have shaped it into the community we see today. Locals trust the authorities to respect the aspirations and identities of the individual communities which comprise the whole of Telford. Donnington, Donnington Wood and Muxton, like the other settlements, have a proud and fascinating history.

Eleven
C & W Walker

C & W Walker's origins were in the firm of Charles Walker & Sons which began trading in Clerkenwell, London, in 1837. The firm specialised in the manufacture of stamps, presses and press tools. In 1857 the works were transferred to Donnington where the founder handed over control to his two sons, Charles Clement and William Thomas Walker, whereupon the partnership was called C & W Walker. Initially the works centred on a blacksmith's forge and made general engineering products with a work force of about thirty-five.

Around 1868 the firm started making large gasholders and purifiers, and as its reputation spread it was able to expand rapidly, acquire more land and consequently enlarge its works. An unusual feature is that most of the buildings were made of corrugated iron; this was because the company's landlord, the Duke of Sutherland (as partner of the Lilleshall Company to whom he had transferred ownership of the land), insisted that any permanent buildings erected must be of such design as to be capable of easy conversion into dwelling houses in the event of the company's collapse.

The company's main office in Station Road was one of the few brick-built premises in the works. As it happened, the company's affairs went from strength to strength but, despite the purchase of the freehold to the land in 1942, it saw no need to alter its general appearance. The office buildings remained almost unchanged throughout their existence.

It was during the early years of expansion, in 1879, that a clock, made of cast iron on a timber subframe, was erected and has since become something of a landmark in the area. So much so that in 1987 it was moved to a specially erected tower in the centre of a roundabout on the newly-constructed A518 Wellington-Newport road which runs along the former railway line. Above the clock was a turret which housed the bell used to notify workers when work was due to commence and end. The bell was later replaced by a loud whining buzzer which could be heard all over the area.

The existence of a railway station on the company's doorstep was a valuable asset in the transport of raw materials to, and finished goods from, the factory. Eventually the company laid its own track within the works, even possessing two of its own engines. William Walker ran the company offices in London while Charles ran the ironworks in Donnington and became an important figure in the area, residing at the Old Hall at Lilleshall.

The company occasionally suffered misfortune. Walter Hales was almost killed in September 1875 while unloading wooden poles from a wagon when they fell on top of him. In December of the same year the saw mill was completely gutted by fire during the night. Watchman Benjamin Worrall sounded the alarm whereupon local residents, many of them employees of the company, did all they could to subdue the flames, without success. The fire engine at Newport arrived and, realising the flames were out of control, directed attention to the surrounding buildings to prevent fire spreading throughout the factory. The Duke of

C. & W. WALKER LTD.

London Office:
Telephone No. 5842
London, Victoria

DONNINGTON, Nr. WELLINGTON, SHROPSHIRE

Donnington Office:
Telephone No. 12
Wellington, Shropshire

LONDON OFFICE: 70 VICTORIA STREET, S.W.1

Designers and Manufacturers of

SPIRALLY-GUIDED GASHOLDERS.
GUIDE-FRAMED GASHOLDERS.
HIGH-PRESSURE GASHOLDERS.
WATERLESS GASHOLDERS.
ORDINARY OXIDE PURIFIERS.
DEEP OXIDE PURIFIERS.
OXIDE HANDLING PLANTS.
GAS HEATERS.
WATER TUBE CONDENSERS.
AIR-COOLED CONDENSERS.
STATIC WASHERS.
ROTARY WASHERS.
SCRUBBERS.
ELECTRO DETARRERS.
RETORT BENCH FITTINGS.

RACK AND PINION GAS VALVES.
DOUBLE FACED GAS VALVES.
MILBOURNE OUTSIDE GAS VALVES FOR
PURIFIERS.
SPECIAL VALVES FOR HOT GAS.
TAR AND LIQUOR VALVES.
STEEL OIL STORAGE TANKS.
PRESSED STEEL TANKS.
CAST IRON WATER AND LIQUOR TANKS.
STEEL CHIMNEYS.
CAST IRON PIPES AND SPECIALS.
LARGE AND SMALL IRON CASTINGS.
STEEL PRESSURE VESSELS.
GAS MAINS.
STEEL BUILDINGS AND TOWERS.

STEEL ORE BUNKERS.
STEEL GRAIN SILOS.
COKE BREAKERS.
SULPHATE OF AMMONIA PLANTS.
AMMONIA CONCENTRATING PLANTS.
SULPHUR RECOVERY PLANTS.
BENZOL RECOVERY AND REFINING PLANTS.
TAR DISTILLING & DEHYDRATING PLANTS.
SPECIAL STEAM-HEATED OVENS FOR FOOD-
STUFFS.
EVAPORATORS AND OTHER PLANT FOR
BEET-SUGAR MANUFACTURE.
OIL REFINING PLANTS.
IRON AND TIMBER PATTERNS.
LEAD WORK.

WELDED AND RIVETED STRUCTURAL WORK OF ALL DESCRIPTIONS.

An advertisement for C & W Walker Ltd from 1949, when an office of the company was located in London to encourage overseas customers; doubtless they didn't have a clue where Donnington was!

The offices of C & W Walker's Midland Iron Works, Station Road, Donnington, c. 1949. The turret clock, now on the roundabout which occupies the position of the former Donnington railway station, can be seen on the right.

Sutherland's private fire engine at Lilleshall Hall arrived too late to be of any use. The fire burnt itself out after almost four hours. Fortunately, the building was insured and the Shropshire & North Wales Assurance Company paid £1,500 for rebuilding work.

William died in 1892, Charles in 1897; through the latter's generosity a charity was created (now administered by the Shropshire County Council) for the furtherance of education in the area. The charity financed the foundation of the Walker Technical College at Hartshill in Oakengates (although it could have been built at Donnington), and partly financed the college in Haybridge Road, Wellington, which also bore his name. Apart from funding the college, the company provided other facilities for the people of Donnington, including a reading room around 1867 which housed over 100 books as well as newspapers; it occupied land immediately west of the present Muxton post office in Wellington Road.

The factory premises were also used during the 1930s as a polling station. Miss Picton Turberville was elected one of the country's first women Members of Parliament; she achieved fame by promoting the law which prevented pregnant women from being hanged.

Key personnel in the success and development of C & W Walker. From left to right, top: Charles Walker (founder of the company) and brothers Charles Clement Walker and William Thomas Walker who were partners in the company before its incorporation in 1899. Bottom: R.J. Milbourne and his son S.M. Milbourne. Both became chairmen of the limited company.

C & W Walker became a limited company in 1899, its first managing director being Mr Featherstone; at that time annual profits were about £8,000, its workforce numbered some 700 and it had gained a worldwide reputation as being foremost in the gas works engineering industry. It was fortunate for the survival of Donnington that, at a time when the traditional employer, the Lilleshall Company, was retracting its local operations, another was rapidly expanding. Walker's maintained the reputation gained in the latter years of the nineteenth century. One of the company's greatest achievements was in 1913 when it undertook the design, manufacture and erection of a $12\frac{1}{2}$ million cubic foot capacity gasholder for the Sidney-based Australian Gas Light Company.

The managing director at that time was R.J. Milbourne who invented a special type of valve for use in gasworks, through which his name became a byword in the engineering world. Later his son Sidney became chairman and managing director of the board, later superseded by Mr G. Lewis; it is under their leadership that the company continued to prosper.

Until the gas industry was nationalised in 1947, the company produced its own gas under the trading name Lilleshall Gas Company and conveyed it to homes and other buildings in Donnington and Lilleshall. In 1908, for example, The Bell Inn and St Matthew's church were connected to the mains supply.

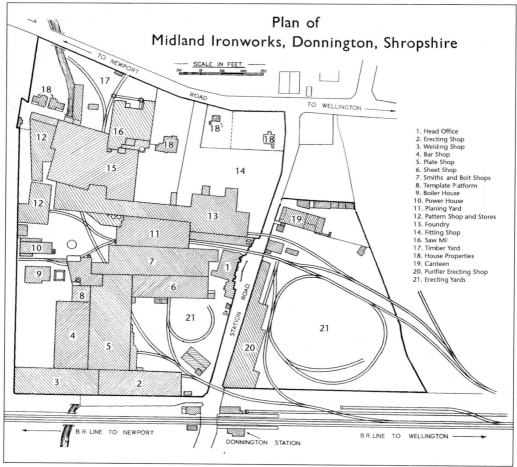

Plan of
Midland Ironworks, Donnington, Shropshire

1. Head Office
2. Erecting Shop
3. Welding Shop
4. Bar Shop
5. Plate Shop
6. Sheet Shop
7. Smiths and Bolt Shops
8. Template Platform
9. Boiler House
10. Power House
11. Planing Yard
12. Pattern Shop and Stores
13. Foundry
14. Fitting Shop
16. Saw Mil
17. Timber Yard
18. House Properties
19. Canteen
20. Purifier Erecting Shop
21. Erecting Yards

A 1949 plan, produced for a booklet commemorating the fiftieth anniversary of the business as a limited company, showing the extent of the Midland Iron Works.

During both World Wars Walkers made steel plates for the ship industry; in the Second World War it manufactured heavy steel shields for large guns, bomb casings, mine destruction gear and other ship and military hardware. The British Government also relied on their expertise for the prompt repair of bomb-damaged gasworks throughout the country.

The company's versatility proved invaluable when natural gas production replaced low-pressure 'town gas', since which time it specialised more in petro-chemical storage containers for gases, liquids and solids. They also produced a wide variety of other items, including sugar containers, silos and welded steel fabrications.

Road transport replaced rail in later years for transporting gigantic products from the factory, partly because of the closure of the main railway line to Stafford (in 1966) and Wellington (in 1969); roads also provided more flexibility of service. Despite increased competition in their particular field of engineering, the company continued to flourish and in 1979 provided work for over 300 people.

C & W Walker's holding company's administration moved to Walker House at Malinslee in September 1979. This heralded the demise of the company's operation in Donnington. Land belonging to the Midland Ironworks was sold to the Telford Development Corporation as a site for smaller industrial concerns in the late 1970s.

C & W Walker's Home Guard platoon, early 1940s. From left to right, back row: C. Talbot, F. Batham, C. Foulkes, H. Bradburne, -?- , R. Millward, M. Lowe, F. Barber, W. Addison, B. Guy. Middle: P. Hicks, A. Rigby, C. Lake, H. Owen, J. James, J. Harris, H. Owen, K. Barber, H. Pickering. Front: J. Mainwaring, C. Williams, G. Guy, A. Winnall, T. Swift, C. Jones (Captain), C. Beech, F. Brown, J. Pugh, -?- , F. Winnall.

C & W Walker's Saw Mill, c. 1953. Women as well as men were employed by the company, especially from the Second World War onwards.

Employees of C & W Walker's with 50 or more years of service to the company, 1949. From left to right, back row: D. Lawley (54 years), C.G. Turner (50), C.T. Fenn (51), J. Edwards (50), B. Pickering (52). Front: G. Talbot (58 years), W. Ellis (57), B. Bott (65), F.C. Franks (68), T.P. Lowe (55), T.H. Brown (52), G. Cooper (53), T. Smith (62).

With hindsight, this was a temporary expedient; the offices and factory premises of C & W Walker Ltd in Station Road were subsequently demolished to make way for new housing and the surrounding roads remodelled, although a short stretch of the original road remains.

As with other aspects of 'progress' in Donnington, older residents feel that no regard seems to have been taken of the historical or social siginificance of the office buildings.

C & W Walker's staff outing, 1958. Chairman and Managing Director Sidney Milbourne is seated, holding his hat, third from the right. Other employees pictured are Harry Lowe, Tom Bott, Eric James, Herbert Davies, Walter Hobson, Ted Pugh, George Cooper, Cecil Lake, J. Brothwood, E. Lowe, J. Martin, John Hayward, Basil Hodge, Rupert Verling, L. Stephens, Cecil Alexander, Harry Brown, Bert Turner, Kath Jones, Joan Norton, Rita Rubery, Mr Chidlow, Frank Johnson, Clarence Stephens.

Following two pages: *Rules and regulations of C & W Walker Ltd, June 1907. 'Persons offending will be severely dealt with…Any inattention to them, absence without leave, sleeping in two mornings in one week, disobedience of orders or general misconduct, will render the Workman liable to dismissal, and the Apprentice to forfeiture of wages, and legal penalties, and the Employers to be sole judges of the rendering of these Rules and Regulations.'*

C. & W. WALKER, Ltd.

RULES AND REGULATIONS FOR ALL WORKMEN, APPRENTICES, AND BOYS, EMPLOYED AT THE MIDLAND IRON WORKS, DONNINGTON, NEAR NEWPORT, SHROPSHIRE.

All Persons are engaged on condition that they observe the following Rules and Regulations. A Copy exhibited at the Time-Keeper's Office, will be held sufficient intimation and legal notice thereof.

The week's work for one week's pay will be 53 hours, as follows:–

From Monday to Friday inclusive:	From	6.0 a.m. to 8.30 a.m.
		9.00 a.m. to 1.0 p.m.
		2.0 p.m. to 5.0 p.m.
Saturday:	From	6.0 a.m. to 8.30 a.m.
		9.0 a.m. to 12.0 noon.

From six in the morning to five o'clock in the afternoon every day, except Saturday, allowing half an hour for breakfast and one hour for dinner, and on Saturday from Six to Twelve o'clock, allowing half an hour for breakfast only.

OVERTIMES.–To be worked when and to the extent required, and will be paid at the rate of two and a half hours for each two hours worked,–a week's time being made before counting overtime, except time is lost from the following reasons;–specified holidays by notice at the Time-office; inability to work by reason of accidents, or repairs to machinery.

PIECE WORK.–All persons engaged on piece work to be subject to these Rules and Regulations, unless excluded by special agreement. All advances on contracts will be made according to time worked at time wages, and the balance paid on completion of the work, except such portions of work are completed so as to be calculated up to Wednesday night previous to pay day.

WAGES.–In payment of wages, any total sum of one half-penny and under will not be paid; any sum over a halfpenny will be counted as 1d. Wages will be paid on leaving off on Saturday (except on Good Friday week and Christmas week, or other special holiday when it will be at the discretion of the employers), and will be paid up to the previous Wednesday night, including the Wednesday's overtime. Piece-work will be paid up to the previous Wednesday night, unless otherwise specially notified by due notice on Notice B and at Time Office. Three days' pay will be kept in hand on every pay day. The pay cards to be put in the baskets before leaving the works, or in case of illness within two days, and if not so returned 3d. will be deducted from next pay. The Turret Clock at Time Office is to be the guide for the division of time.

CHECKING AND BELL RINGING.–Every person will receive 4 checks, free of charge, on entering his engagements, to be given up on leaving it. Should he lose any, others will be supplied, and 3d. each stopped from his wages.

One check is to be deposited in check box on coming to work in the morning, another on coming in after breakfast, and the third on coming in after dinner, and the fourth to be used when working overtime, to be put in check box when leaving the works; the four will be returned to him before leaving off work each day, and anyone leaving without his checks will have his time stopped from previous checking. Persons working half-hour dinner will not be allowed to check before 1.25, and those working the whole of the meal-time must check within Five minutes after the Bell has rung for leaving off work.

The time boxes for receiving the checks will remain open for fifteen minutes, and will be closed one minute before the time for commencing work, except at 6 a.m. The bell will be rung five minutes before, and again at one minute before each time of commencing work, except at 6 a.m., as a signal that the check box is closed, by which time all checks must be deposited in the check box: and three strokes of the bell will be given at six, nine, and two o'clock, when every person must be at and commence his work.

COMING LATE.–Should any person arrive after the check box is closed at six in the morning, the box at the time-keeper's office will be opened to receive his check from 6.25 to 6.30, when it will be closed, and such person loses half-an-hour. No person will be allowed to commence work at any other time without special permission from his foreman.

MEDICAL EXAMINATION.–Each boy or youth, coming under the Factory Act, will be stopped 3d., towards the cost of Medical Inspection, on the following Saturday after employment.

HOLIDAYS.–Whatever holidays are permitted due notice of same will be placed at the time-keeper's office.

MEALS.–All employees except those specially ordered to work during meal times, must leave the works within five minutes after the bell has rung. A mess room is provided, and it is intended all should go there and not remain in the works. Persons working all night are allowed from 9 to 9.30 o'clock for meal-time, and may remain in the works.

NOTICE TO LEAVE.–Every person on being discharged, except for misconduct, will receive a week's notice from any pay day. Any person wishing to leave his employment must give a week's notice, in writing, to his foreman, from any pay day, at the termination of which notice the three days' pay in hand will be paid. Any person leaving his employment without the proper notice named will forfeit the three days' pay in hand, and render himself liable to legal consequences. No persons allowed to take any box, parcel, wisket, basket or bag into or out of the works.

INJURING TOOLS, &c.–Any person, by neglect or carelessness, injuring tools, machinery, buildings, drawings, or other property of his employers, will be liable to be charged with cost of repairing the same in liquidation of damages, the amount to be deducted from his wages.

WORKMEN RESPONSIBLE FOR THEIR TOOLS.–Every person will be held responsible for the portable tools delivered to him by the storekeeper or foreman, and for the fixed tools he may be working with. All tools must be kept clean and in good order, and the portable ones returned when done with.

MACHINES TO BE KEPT CLEAN.–Persons at machines are to keep their machines clean and properly lubricated; but no gearing or other moving parts are to be cleaned while the machine is in motion. To clean such parts fifteen minutes will be allowed before closing on Saturday, which time must be employed for that purpose alone.

ACCIDENTS TO BE GUARDED AGAINST.–As it is essential to guard against accidents, and to reduce them as far as practicable to a minimum, all foremen and others in authority are directed to caution any persons whom they see exposing themselves unnecessarily to such risks; and any person who, through his carelessness or neglect at work, appears likely to involve himself or his fellow workmen, or render them liable to accident, is to be at once discharged.

NO STRANGERS TO BE ADMITTED.–No strangers are to be admitted to the works.

No persons allowed to go out of the works during work hours without special permission of their foreman.

FINES.–Fines will be enforced for certain offences as under.

Any apprentice absenting himself without leave, will forfeit double his wages, and if found loitering about, and not attending to his work with due diligence, will be stopped 3d. each time from his wages, and in all cases be subject to legal penalties.

Putting coat on, or leaving work before bell rings...	0s. 6d
Washing the hands in oil, without the special leave of the foreman or otherwise wasting or making an improper use of it; or wasting candles...	1s. 0d
Taking wood for lighting fires from any other place than that marked out by the foreman of the Saw Mill...	1s. 0d
Trampling with dirty boots about sawn timber and planks...	1s. 0d
Breaking open the lock of another workman's box or drawer, or removing tools from a bench or machine without permission...	1s. 0d. to 2s. 0d
Removing a burner from gas light or using the same with burner removed, without at once informing the foreman for first offence...	0s. 6d
for each subsequent offence...	1s. 0d
Entering or leaving the works by any other than the entrance at the time-office (except at 3.30 and 5 o'clock, and then only by one gate in the Newport Road, which is opened solely for the convenience of the men)...	0s. 6d
Going out of the works during work hours without leave...	1s. 0d
Going out of the works after check is put into box and before the bell rings for commencing work	0s. 3d
Putting any other person's check or checks into the box; and the person whose check is so put into the box...	1s. 0d
Second offence... 2s. 0d. and immediate dismissal.	
Taking other persons' checks...	1s. 0d
Second offence... 2s. 0d. and immediate dismissal.	
Throwing at, or otherwise annoying other persons...	2s. 0d
Firing off guns, or explosives of any kind... 5s. 0d. and immediate dismissal.	
Riotous or noisy conduct of any kind is not permitted, and if persisted in after being cautioned, the person will be fined...	1s. 0d
Any person sending for, or bringing in beer or spirits without special leave from the foreman in writing...	2s. 0d
All pipes to be put out before passing check box, and any man found smoking in the works...	3s. 0d
Staying in works for meals without permission First offence...	1s. 0d
Second offence... 2s. 6d. and dismissal.	
Not checking in accordance with rule First offence...	1s. 0d
Second offence... 2s. 6d. and dismissal.	

Boys and apprentices will be fined one-half of the above amounts.

It is particularly requested that no person will eat his food in front of the offices, or in the station road, or loiter in same, or annoy the public in any way when making use of the road during meal times. Persons offending will be severely dealt with.

C & W Walker Ltd trade advertisement, c. 1949. By this time the company had gained an enviable reputation for innovation and quality. Its massive structures, mainly in the form of gas holders and associated installations, were exported across the world.

Twelve
Religious Activities

From the seventh century, Lilleshall parish church was the religious centre for nearby Donnington and Muxton folk. Rapid population growth during the eighteenth and early nineteenth centuries in areas previously uninhabited meant that many parishioners were too far from Lilleshall to attend services. The Church Commissioners were unable to authorise the building of new churches and had to rely on the voluntary erection of small 'chapels of ease' by local landowners and ironmasters.

The chapel dedicated to St George at Pains Lane was paid for by the Marquis of Stafford in 1806, in what was then part of Donnington Wood. It seems to have been named in memory of St George Leveson Gower, the Marquis's son. The chapel proved insufficient for local needs as it was still too far from the growing Donnington and Donnington Wood populations. The chapel was rebuilt in 1860 with funds provided by the Marquis of Stafford and Isaac Hawkins Browne, a local landowner, and a new parish, also called St Georges, was created in 1861.

Religion was something everyone believed in but seldom had the energy to put into practice. Walking to the parish church at Lilleshall was too much of an effort for many except when someone married or had to be buried. New forms of worship were beginning; nonconformist sects preached an uncompromising gospel far removed from the perceived cosiness and arrogance of the Anglican Church. Religious meetings began, initially in homes or on the pit mounds. In 1814, the home of John Barnet at Donnington was licensed for dissenting worshippers. Similarly, the home of Michael Wilkes in Donnington Wood was licensed in July 1821 as was that of John Norton in January 1822. A Free Methodist chapel at Waxhill Barracks also received a licence in 1822.

The Baptists built their first church in Donnington Wood in 1820 at the southern end of Donnington Barracks (now School Road). As with other nonconformist groups, members had previously met at domestic dwellings until such time as collections and promises of money were forthcoming which enabled them to erect premises specifically for worship. The Baptist movement was one of the foremost in Donnington Wood; various divisions of Methodism soon followed. Ironically, considering how they were viewed by many, chartermasters often held responsible positions at these 'church' meetings. Attendance at one of the Sunday services became almost obligatory, an aspect of life which was to continue until the mid-twentieth century. The nonconformist message gave comfort in an uncompromising, hostile world.

Methodism, unconstrained by parish boundaries, grew through the fervour with which its evangelists carried out their missionary work. Revivalist meetings on the hillsides and even in the furnaces attracted huge crowds; over 4,000 attended an open air gathering led by the Primitive Methodists on the Cinder Hill in 1839. Methodism in its various forms was the most popular of teachings on the coalfield, appealing as it did to the deep emotional needs of people

The original Baptist church of 1820 with subsequent additions, 1950. The church closed in 1968 when a new one was built in Queens Road.

In 1806, the first church to be built in Donnington Wood was erected along Pain's Lane which became part of the newly created St Georges parish in 1861. This contemporary illustration shows what the church, built as a chapel of ease, looked like.

Gilbert Scott, 1811-1878, architect of St Matthew's parish church, Donnington Wood.

living in a dangerous and difficult environment.

Acts of Parliament in 1818, 1835 and 1843 enabled the Established Church to create new parishes and provided financial aid for the erection of churches in the newer centres of population. The Duke of Sutherland, concerned as he was for morality on his estates, built the church dedicated to St Matthew at Donnington Wood in 1845 to promote 'the interests of religion and to give spiritual advantage to certain of the inhabitants...who reside at an inconvenient distance' from Lilleshall and Pains Lane churches.

The architect was Gilbert Scott, born in Buckinghamshire in 1811. By the time he died in 1878 (through overwork), he had achieved an astounding production of about 800 buildings. He is buried in Westminster Abbey. During his lifetime he received many honours, including a knighthood in 1872. By the late 1840s he had gained a reputation as one of the foremost architects of church design in the Neo-Gothic style which was undergoing a national revival at that time. It is no surprise, therefore, that the Duke of Sutherland appointed him for the design of the church at Donnington Wood.

Several of Scott's buildings and restorations survive. Although the church of St Matthew is the only one in Telford, there are other examples of his work to be found in Shropshire, particularly the restorations to the church of St Lawrence at Ludlow. The restoration of the Chapter House in Westminster Abbey and the Prince Albert Memorial were also designed by Scott, as were the comprehensive plans for the restoration of the whole of Lichfield Cathedral which lasted from 1856 to 1908. The church of St Matthew can be regarded as an early stage in the career of a most distinguished Victorian architect. It is interesting to note that Scott's grandson, Sir Giles Gilbert Scott (1880-1960) designed and is buried in the Anglican Cathedral at Liverpool.

The Duke allocated £2,000 for the church; in fact it appears to have cost about £1,875, and because of the price limit was fitted with a bellcote instead of a tower. The church was sited on the 'Occupational Road leading from the Turnpike Road to the Lilleshall Navigable Canal' and was 'to be equipped with a decent communion table and rails, the requisite plate for the celebration of the Holy Sacrament', a reading desk, wooden pulpit, font, bell and seats for 480 persons. An unusual feature was that all the seats were to be 'free'; in most other churches at that time many seats were rented to local families and made up part of the incumbent's income.

No organ was installed but it seems that a harmonium was obtained in 1863. An organ was installed in 1866 at a cost of £210 to replace the harmonium. After numerous overhauls and repairs it was replaced by the present organ in 1974.

The bell weighs 2cwt. Hung in 1953 at a cost of £95, it is appropriately inscribed 'Coronation 1953'. The previous bell, rather smaller, was sold to the bellfoundry for re-smelting. The churchyard gate was originally of cast iron made in the local furnace and was replaced by a wooden one in 1885. Oak double gates were later erected and the path widened in 1966 to give access to motor vehicles direct to the front door. Initially the church appears to have been centrally heated with coal donated by the Lilleshall Company, and lit by oil lamps and candles. A gas pipeline was laid by the Lilleshall Gas Company in 1908, and since then various types of heating and lighting appliances have been employed. At present electricity is used and seems to be less troublesome than its predecessors.

Successive dukes arranged and paid for such repairs as were necessary, using workers from the Lilleshall Company, but by far the largest structural alterations took place in the mid-1960s, when the Wellington architect, Lesley B. Byram, was commissioned to design extensions to the building, including a choir vestry and baptistry using identical Grinshill stone from the ruins of Lodge Furnaces. Cyril Nicholls (then Secretary of the Lilleshall Company) and J. Brass (Divisional Chairman of the National Coal Board) laid the foundation stones; the former represented the company which originally built the furnaces, the latter the present owners of the land upon which the furnace remains still stood.

Once created, the churchyard became the cemetery for Donnington folk; funerals no longer needed to be at Lilleshall. The first Nonconformist funeral took place there in 1891.

Apart from the obvious links with the local Church of England aided or controlled schools, St Matthew's has been closely involved with the Cub/Scout and Brownie/Guide

Watercolour painting of St Matthew's parish church, Donnington Wood, c. 1900. During the 1960s the church was enlarged and the gateway widened to allow vehicles to drive up to the porch.

movements, the Royal British Legion and the Royal Regiment of Artillery. At one time it ran a youth club, but changing social attitudes caused its closure.

The original vicarage, adjacent to the White House Hotel, is a white-painted timber-framed building with an unusual canopied porch and is probably of Tudor origin, once used as a farmhouse for one of the Leveson tenants. The vicarage was granted to the Living in 1850 and, when Sir George Grey, Home Secretary, notified the Duke and curate that Donnington Wood had been granted parish status in 1851, it remained the residence of the Donnington incumbent until the 1980s (when a new house in St Georges Road was obtained) even though it lay within the Lilleshall parish.

Before the building of the Church Institute in 1901, the vicarage was host to a variety of functions, including tea-parties, feasts and fêtes for the benefit of parishioners and schoolchildren. In 1920 it was purchased by Sir John Leigh, Baronet, upon the dispersal of the Lilleshall Estates, and was subsequently bought by the diocese in 1926.

In 1846 the United Methodists built a chapel (many Methodists preferred the word chapel because 'churches' were strongly associated with the Anglican religion) at the northern end of Donnington Barracks, partly of bricks made at the brickworks behind The Bell Inn. It was lit by gas from the Lilleshall Gas Company until 1950 when electricity was installed. For many years it ran gymnastic classes and was used as a clinic. It closed in 1966 although the premises were still used as a Sunday school for some time afterwards..

Religious activities continued to grow throughout the remainder of the century. In 1866, after several years of Sunday cottage services, a Primitive Methodist chapel was built near the Coal Wharf at a cost of £503 18s 11d; the seating was for 300 and some 200 people attended regularly, 220 of the seats were rented. Many Methodist chapels were given

St Matthew's original vicarage, Wellington Road, Donnington, 1979.

St Matthew's church hall, Donnington Wood. The 1920s photograph, below, shows what the original building looked like. At that time it was referred to simply as The Institute and hosted a wide variety of church events. During the 1960s, the building was given a new entrance, better catering facilities and extended at the rear to provide a greatly enlarged hall complete with raised stage. Traces of the original larger side window could still be seen, as shown above, in 1979. The hall was sold in the late 1990s; the front has since been demolished and the hall at the rear converted into a vehicle testing centre.

dedication names; that at the Coal Wharf was called Ebenezer, which means 'the stone of help'. By the 1890s a small orchestra, comprising Arthur Hill (violin), Joel Lake (clarinet), Bob Robinson (cornet and organ), Alex and George Fryer (cello and double bass) and others, accompanied the singing.

A Sunday school was erected at the back of the chapel in 1884 to compete with that already functioning at the Anglican church. Charles Walker and J. Pownall laid the foundation stones. Children who were absent from Sunday school could expect a visit from one of the teachers to ascertain the reason. Sunday school anniversaries (expected entertainment in most Methodist chapels) became dreaded events for performing children but proud moments for their parents.

The Wesleyan Methodists built their chapel on the main road near Furnace Lane around 1870. In 1905, a breakaway sect of Wrockwardine Wood Methodists took over the red-roofed, corrugated-iron clad Central Hall on the Cinder Hill, which had originally been built as an isolation hospital during an epidemic a few years earlier. Before its demolition during the 1980s it was claimed to have the best sounding organ in the Midlands.

One of the appealing aspects of Nonconformism was that it relied heavily on lay preachers, such as William Latham who terrorised the Baptist congregation with exhortations that when 'gross darkness fell over the face of the earth, it was the equal of 144 times of the greatest pit darkness'. Only miners familiar with conditions inside the pits could appreciate how dark that must be.

William was not just a local preacher; he was also a fanatical leader of the Miners Union. The Shropshire Committee of the Union waged a bitter struggle against the Lilleshall Company in 1913 for better conditions and wages. A strike was called but ultimately doomed to failure. The churches and chapels gave support by providing food for hungry children (the Baptists alone fed some 100 children with soup and bread every day for the duration).

The mission room (or church) of St Chad, a corrugated iron structure, was erected between the former Lodgebank and Barnyard mines, not far from the Granville mine, around 1888 and was of a similar design to the mission room at Muxton. It was intended to serve as a chapel of ease for Anglicans residing in that area but never achieved much success; it closed during the Second World War. It reopened in March 1957 with an enthusiastic new congregation but eventually attendance levels fell again. It was dismantled and subsequently reassembled in the Blists Hill Museum.

The next church to be built was not until the early 1940s when the Roman Catholics opened a small building near Barclay Lodge. Attendance increased so that a new church became necessary and was built in Winifred's Drive in 1945, whereupon the previous premises were acquired by the Serbian Orthodox (Yugoslavian Diocese) congregation to serve the needs of a rising population of refugees from Eastern Europe. COD Donnington also built the multi-denominational Memorial Church of the Holy Trinity at The Humbers end of their site. It is unusual in that it has loudspeakers mounted on its tower through which amplified pre-recorded bell peals can be played.

The 1960s witnessed a new era in church-building activities. In 1965 St Matthew's church hall was extended as the original institute, erected in 1901 and opened by the Duchess of Sutherland, was totally inadequate. In 1967 extensions to the church itself were completed, and in May of the same year the three Methodist chapels combined to form a single congregation at a new church in Wrekin Drive at a cost of £26,000; its car park is on the site of a temporary wooden chapel which had been erected in 1948-49.

The Unitarian chapel was demolished and the Wesleyan chapel taken over by Staffordshire Farmers Ltd; it was demolished to make way for a car sales business. The Primitive Methodist chapel at the Coal Wharf is now used by the Serbian Orthodox (USA-Canadian Diocese). The year 1967 also saw work begin on the new Roman Catholic church dedicated to Our Lady of the Rosary; upon its completion the previous temporary church

St Matthew's church choir, c. 1928. Choirmaster Walter Hobson, who also led the Donnington Wood Institute Male Voice Choir, is seated in the centre.

Mission room (or church) of St Chad, erected c. 1888. The church closed during the 1940s; this is the congregation when it reopened in 1957. The church managed to survive until the 1970s after which it was dismantled and re-erected at the Blists Hill Museum.

Central Hall, which stood on waste ground at the southern end of Furnace Lane, 1979.

Former Primitive Methodist chapel at the Coal Wharf, now a Serbian Orthodox church, 1965.

United Methodist church, School Road, c. 1930.

Methodist church, Wrekin Drive, 1979.

Serbian Orthodox church at Barclay Court, 1979.

Our Lady of the Rosary Catholic church, 1979.

Baptist church in Queens Road, 1979.

Memorial Church of the Holy Trinity, 1979.

was converted to a social club. At the time of writing, the future of a Roman Catholic church in Donnington is in doubt; owing to the poor state of the building, Our Lady of the Rosary was demolished in 2001.

A new Baptist church was built in November 1968 on land once used by Brown's bus company to park its vehicles. Its first service took place in September 1969. The church stands only a few metres away from the original chapel (last renovated in 1906) which has since been used as a joinery centre and for other commercial activities.

MEN OF THIS PARISH WHO FELL IN GREAT WAR 1914 - 1918

C. B. DAKIN	J. LEESE
J. CLEMSON	W. MANSELL
W. A. COOPER	J. MASSEY
J. COTTON	G. MULLINDER
J. EDWARDS	B. RIGBY
V. FLETCHER	H. SAVAGE
. FOULKES	W. TATLOR
A. HAYWARD	R. THOMPSON
L. G. HOPE	W. TRANTER
J. LATHAM	W. WAKELEY
R. D. LEES	N. R. W. WILLIAMS

MEN OF THIS PARISH WHO FELL IN THE GREAT WAR 1939 - 1945

A. N. CLEMSON	A. EDWARDS
J. E. FAKE	R. A. GAUT
M. HEYES	G. J. LAWLEY
J. LEACH	J. T. LONGSTAFF
A. P. McGREGOR	G. R. NORTON
G. A. OLIVER	W. J. PICKERING
W. E. PYE	H. SHORE
G. R. STEVENSON	J. N. WHITEHOUS

Two war memorial plaques cast in steel and set into the wall on either side of the memorial gates at the entrance to the School Road Recreation Grounds. Many of the surnames have long-standing associations with Donnington and Donnington Wood. A war memorial garden was also laid out at a road intersection near Winifreds Drive shortly after the Second World War.

Thirteen

Education

The first school was erected in the 1840s next to St Matthew's church and was known as the Donnington Wood National School. Before then, children could attend the school at Lilleshall for a halfpenny a day but regular attendance was rare. The Donnington Wood school was paid for and patronised by the Duke of Sutherland. His decision to build it may have been influenced by the 1837/38 report made by the Commons' Select Committee on the Education of the Poorer Classes which found 'that the kind of education given to the children of the working classes is lamentably deficient'. Isaac Perry and Miss Edith Bradnor were the first head teachers.

The village school eventually became known as the Duke of Sutherland's school, a name kept until the early 1900s. The school provided an elementary education for children of both sexes and all ages; in 1854 it split into two separate sections, boys and infants, and older girls. Owing to an increasing population, application was made for a separate infants' school in 1867, but this was not achieved until 1893. Attendance was voluntary (as it was nationally) until the 1880 Education Act. However, children attending the school were given special treats by the Duke, such as trips to Lilleshall Abbey and Hall (via tub-boats on the canal) and the Wrekin (in horse-drawn wagonettes supplied by the Lilleshall Company) as well as 'feasts' to celebrate marriages and births in the Sutherland family.

When local government widened its powers the Duke's influence was reduced, although the Church of England retained control of certain school activities as it has done since the beginning. Head teachers in the 1920s were Walter Perry and Miss Franklin. In 1933 the infants and girls schools amalgamated.

The arrival of the Central Ordnance Depot in 1939 brought a large number of people into the area and the school became very overcrowded. The Wrockwardine Wood Senior School was built to relieve the situation at Donnington Wood, which then became a mixed junior and infants school with only one head teacher.

In September 1949, owing to further increases in child population, the infants were transferred to the new Donnington County Infants' School (in Baldwin Webb Avenue) which increased its pupil population from 70 to 286 by July 1979.

During the 1950s and 1960s the Donnington Wood Junior School, again owing to further increases, had to find accommodation for the rising number of pupils, so in 1954 the annexe was opened near to the County Infants' School, having previously been used as a wartime nursery school for working mothers. In the late 1960s and early 1970s the annexe was used as a special school for handicapped children and in 1975 became a nursery school again.

In July 1966 the Donnington Wood Church of England Primary School was dedicated by the Lord Bishop of Lichfield (in whose diocese Donnington lies); the old Donnington Wood School became an annexe to the new school, which catered for as many children as it did when it was first opened in June 1965.

The National School, now demolished, stood next to St Matthew's church.

Girls cookery class of 1930/31. The national school had no facilities for teaching such a vital subject so the class was obliged to walk to St Georges Institute and use the equipment there. From left to right, back row: Nellie Carr, Mabel Dyke, Vera Downing, Clara Lawley, Sarah Naylor, Sylvia Smith, Gwen Williams, Flossie Hicks, Olive Wagg. Second row: Edith Carr, Agnes Leese, Nancy Palin, Maud Speed, Irene Cooper, Daisy Leek, Nora Brothwood, Joyce Cooper, Winnie Owen. The headmistress was Miss Hughes (right) who lived in Shrewsbury but lodged at Donnington Wood Farm during the school week. Third row: Bessie Meredith, Dolly Oliver, Marjorie Millward, Elsie Pickering, Emma Doody, Eileen Pritchard, Eira Colley, Edna Morgan, Joan White. Front row: Gwen White, Gwen Bradburn, Betty Johnson.

118

In May 1972 St Matthew's Church of England Aided School (not 'controlled' like the other Church of England school) was dedicated by the Lord Bishop of Lichfield and has about 300 pupils. It is situated a few yards to the south-east of the church and serves the needs of the nearby council and private housing estates, the former erected rather speedily by Second City Homes during the early 1970s, the latter by a variety of house-building companies during the 1990s for the private market.

The original National School buildings were demolished during the 1990s as they were no longer required for educational purposes. Many children living in Donnington during the 1970s and 1980s attended The John Hunt School in Gibbons Road, just outside Donnington's western boundary at Furnace Lane. It had previously been called Trench Modern School. Having gained something of a poor reputation for its educational standards and discipline, it has been given a new lease of life and a new title: The Sutherland School. The current name provides a link with the history of the area.

DONNINGTON WOOD
CORONATION SPORTS.

Programme of Events.

Ages	Distance or Race	BOYS PRIZES.				GIRLS PRIZES.		
		1st.	2nd	3rd.		1st.	2nd.	3rd.
7 and 8	100yds.	2/-	1/6	1/-	...	2/-	1/6	1/-
9 and 10	100yds.	2/6	1/6	1/-	...	2/6	1/6	1/-
11 to 14	100yds.	3/-	2/-	1/-	...	3/-	2/-	1/-
7 to 14	Obstacle Race ...	3/-	2/-					
7 to 14	Sack Race ...	3/-	2/-					
7 to 14	Skipping Race ...				...	2/6	1/6	
7 to 14	Egg and Spoon Race				...	2/6	1/6	

Jumping, open to any Boy who has not left School.

	1st.	2nd.			1st.	2nd.
High Jump ...	2/6	1/6	...	Standard Jump	2/6	1/6

Open to any Girl who has not left School.

	1st.	2nd.	3rd.
For the most Fancy Dress Worn on Coronation Day	5/-	3/-	2/-

Cutting the Fowl down, Blindfolded, Open to any Boy or Girl not over 14 years.

Races for Boys and Girls under 7 years will be arranged on the ground and suitable prizes (NOT CASH) will be presented, Value £1.

Programme of events for children taking part in the 1911 Coronation sports.

DONNINGTON FIND IS DECLARED "TREASURE TROVE"
JURY'S DECISION AT UNUSUAL WELLINGTON INQUEST

OVER 500 ANCIENT SILVER COINS ON VIEW WELLINGTON Urban Council Chamber was the scene of an unusual "inquest" on Wednesday, when Mr. J. V. T. Lander, the Wellington and District coroner, sat with eight "good and lawful men, duly chosen", to inquire into the finding of ancient treasure by a workman when engaged on excavation work in a garden, once allotted to No. 18, Wellington Road, Donnington. The workman, Fredk. Jones, of No. 207, Trench, who is employed by Messrs. John France and Son, Ltd., was preparing a trench for building purposes, when his pick struck an earthenware urn containing over 500 silver coins of ancient times – dating from 1553 to 1658. The facts were duly reported to the coroner, who, as representative of the King, has to hold an inquiry into the "find" and to obtain a jury's verdict as to whether the "find" is treasure trove.

Big Questions After the coroner had given details as to how the coins were found, and the reasons why it was necessary for him to hold an inquiry – the duty of the jury was to give their verdict as to whether the coinage was treasure trove – he submitted six questions to the jury to answer: What did the find consist of? Where was the find deposited? Was it intentionally hidden, concealed, or accidentally or purposely abandoned? Is the owner unknown? Who is the finder? Did the finder conceal his find?

The questions were eventually duly answered, the jury agreeing that they were treasure trove; that they were intentionally hidden; that the owner was unknown; that the finder was Fred Jones; and that he did not conceal his find, etc. The inquisition, signed by the chairman and each member of the jury, included the following passage:–"That the treasure so found was of ancient times, viz. between the period of 1553 and 1658, deposited, hidden and concealed... that the owner or owners cannot be found, and is therefore treasure trove and the property of our said Lord the King, and that it be handed to His Majesty's treasurer on behalf of our said Lord the King, which said treasure trove I, the said coroner, have taken and seized in His Majesty's hands." The coins were exhibited and inspected by the jury, as was the broken urn which had contained them.

Details of Coinage At the outset of the inquiry, the coroner referred to its unusual nature and went on to give details of the coins, numbering 517. The first coin shown to the jury was one of the reign of Queen Mary 1st, the coroner remarking that there was only one Philip and Mary coin in the collection. Next, the coroner mentioned that there were 300 coins of the reign of Queen Elizabeth (1558 - 1603), and he then exhibited 135 coins of James 1st reign (1603 - 1625), and then the remainder of Charles 1st reign. The coroner said that it was quite reasonable to imagine that the coins were deposited in the ground by some person during the reign of Charles 1st who was beheaded – and the days of Cromwell, to prevent them from being taken. Mr. France did the right thing in reporting the matter to him after the workman had reported the find to Mr. France. "I shall now call certain evidence," continued the coroner, "and it will be for you to return your verdict." Evidence was then called.

Traced Back For 130 Years The first witness was Sgt. Harrison (Newport), who said that having received information of the find he visited the garden adjoining No.18, Wellington Road, Donnington, and the occupiers had been traced back for something like 130 years. The present tenant was Mr. Harry Rubery, and Mrs. Rubery was a daughter of Mrs. Vandrill, who occupied the Post Office at Donnington. She was an invalid, but he had had a conversation with her. She was born at No. 18, and her grandmother was born in the same house. Sgt. Harrison said he gathered from the conversation that the cottages were originally a farm house.

"It's Money!" Mr. John France, builder and contractor, Trench, said that on March 22 his bricklayer, Frederick Jones, brought the coins to him in his cap. Jones remarked, "I have got something here, don't be afraid, it's money!" Witness then saw that they were ancient coins. The trench from which were recovered was about 18 inches deep. Witness added that he bought the cottages and the garden at the Duke of Sutherland's sale and in 1919 he conveyed the property to his wife.

Workman's Story Fredk. Jones, the workman, said he was getting out the foundations for two houses when his pick struck something in the ground. "It did not sound like an old drain pipe," he said, "and I bent down and got the coins out in my hand... I found that there was more than I could get in my hand so I put them in my hat. I did not know what coins they were, but saw that there were several hundreds, and I took them in my cap to Mr. France." The coroner: The ground could not have been disturbed for many years? – No. Harry Rubery, who lives at No. 18, the cottage adjoining the garden, said the garden had been cultivated regularly up to the last 10 years. The piece of ground where the coins were found had not been cultivated at all for that period. Mrs. Rubery, wife of the previous witness, said she had lived at No. 18 for 45 years. Her mother was born in the cottage. Her (witness's) grandmother had spoken of her grandmother having lived at the cottage. The coroner: The cottage has been in the occupation of your family for nearly 200 years? – Yes, it must have been. The coroner said that that was all the evidence he had to put to the jury, and he went on to detail the questions he had put to the jury. After the jury had returned their verdict, the coroner thanked the jury for their attendance. It was an unusual inquest and he had not known a similar one for the last 50 years.

Fourteen

Donnington Treasure

No history of Donnington would be complete without the mention of a hoard of treasure discovered in March 1938 by a workman digging out the foundations of the house now aptly named Treasure Trove Villa next to the old Primitive Methodist chapel.

A total of 517 coins were found, with dates ranging from the reigns of Queen Mary (1554) to King Charles I (1642). Of the coins, 300 belonged to the reign of Queen Elizabeth I comprising silver pennies and other denominations up to five shilling pieces. They had been placed in an earthenware pot which was mistakenly reported as being Roman in origin and led to a misconception that they were Roman coins inside. A Coroner's Inquest declared them to be Treasure Trove and compensated the finder from public funds.

It seems likely that the coins were hidden during 1643 while Lilleshall Abbey was under siege by Parliamentary troops. From this we can assume that the depositor either did not trust them and believed that it would be taken from him as plunder, or was himself a Royalist supporter in which case his possessions could have been seized anyway. Whatever the reason, he must have perished during the strife as he did not return to recover the cache. Considering the amount involved it is unlikely that he would have left it buried if he had had any choice in the matter.

The discovery caused quite a stir at the time and prompted a diviner from St Georges, Samuel Bloor (a grocer in Gower Street), armed with his hazel twigs, to pass over other parts of Donnington in search of 'influences'. He was confident that more treasure lay hidden underground in the area.

In recent years, metal detectorists have found many pit and public house tokens scattered around the old pit workings, but so far no one has discovered another pot of treasure…

Opposite: *The Treasure Trove inquest as reported by* The Wellington Journal & Shrewsbury News, *2 April 1938.*

Fifteen
Sir Gordon Richards

Donnington's most renowned inhabitant of the twentieth century, Gordon Richards, was born on 5 May 1904. As a child he lived in Ivy Row (sometimes called Potato Row), a group of now-demolished colliers' cottages owned by the Lilleshall Company, near the present Richards House in Cordingley Way.

His mother, Elizabeth, was a dressmaker and his father Nathan tended the horses belonging to the Granville pit. Gordon had ample opportunity to ride them in his youth.

On leaving the Donnington Wood National School, he worked as a clerk to the Lilleshall Company until 1919 when he left to train as a stable apprentice for Martin Hartigan at Foxhill, near Swindon. Before long he was racing horses for the stables and was named 'Jockey of the Year' for the first time in 1925, a title he attained a total of twenty-six times during his career. His first win was on Gay Lord at Leicester in 1921.

In 1947 he rode a staggering 269 winners, and rode over 200 winners in a season on 12 further occasions. He rode his 4,000th winner in 1950 and his 4,500th in 1952 when he broke the world record. Six days before he received his knighthood in 1953, he won the Coronation Derby riding Pinza. He retired from racing after a serious fall while leaving the paddock at Sandown Park in 1954, having ridden a total of 4,870 winners out of 21,834 races during his career.

He subsequently began a new career as a trainer, with limited success. In 1970 he retired from training to become racing manager to Lady Beaverbrook and Sir Michael Sobell. He died, aged 82, on 10 November 1986, at his home in Kintbury, Berkshire.

The 'Champion Jockey' public house is named after him, as is Richards House.

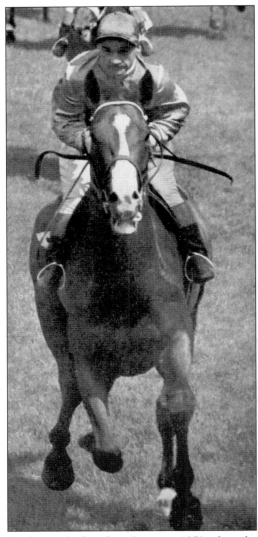

Gordon Richards riding Pinza in 1953, from his autobiography, My Life, *published by Hodder & Stoughton in 1955.*

Sixteen

Muxton

Until fairly recent times, Muxton was largely untouched by the historical developments which affected neighbouring Donnington. As with many English villages, its origins probably date back to Saxon times. In 1086 it was known as Mokelston, in 1100 Mukleston and in 1240 as Mokleston. Other variations are recorded until it became known as Muxton.

There has been some speculation about how the name is derived. The most feasible is from 'mucs', a corruption of the Saxon word for swine, and 'ton', a farm. The Welsh 'mochros' means swine moor, the inference being that pigs were reared here before the Norman conquest. Muxton formed part of the Lilleshall Abbey estate and would have provided food and services for the canons. An alternative derivation may be that the settlement was named after a Saxon called Mucel who had a farm in the area.

Muxton had very few dwellings and, in fact, occupied very little land until local councils altered boundaries during the twentieth century. As in Donnington and Donnington Wood, the surrounding fields had names to make them easily identifiable.

Historically, Muxton began opposite the site of old The Sutherland Arms public house on the old Wellington-Newport Road and included land confined to both sides of Muxton Lane as well as fields to the east towards Honnington. It certainly did not include any other part of Wellington Road which, in fact, formed the original Donnington. Consequently, Muxton comprised very few properties, perhaps the most important of which were Muxton Farm, which may have its foundations in Medieval times, and Muxtonbridge Farm, some of whose buildings have been incorporated into The Shropshire Golf and Country Club. Both appear to include brickwork dating from the late eighteenth to mid-nineteenth century. This would most likely be as a result of the improvements in farming, including new buildings, which occurred during that period. Before it was acquired by the golf club, Muxtonbridge Farm took its name from a bridge which crossed over the canal. The bridge was removed after the canal fell into disuse and silted up in the 1920s.

Other cottages in Muxton were probably occupied by yeoman farmers, farm labourers and a few essential skilled hands at various times throughout the village's history. Inventories taken during the seventeenth to eighteenth centuries confirm this view. John Shelton of ye Walnut Tree died in 1680 leaving a herd of thirty-six cattle of varying ages and both sexes, five horses, twenty sheep, several pigs and chickens. His estate was valued at £291, indicating that he was reasonably affluent for his class. Another yeoman, William Hall who died in 1702, had seventy-seven sheep and a few cattle and horses. His estate was valued at £154. Not all yeoman farmers did so well: Richard Hawkins also died in 1702 and left assets worth £54. Unfortunately he also had debts amounting to £40. Another John Shelton (died 1707) left an estate worth £431. His widow Philippa kept the farm for a little over a year until she also died, at which time the value had fallen to £211. Presumably some of her husband's assets had been given to relatives in the interim.

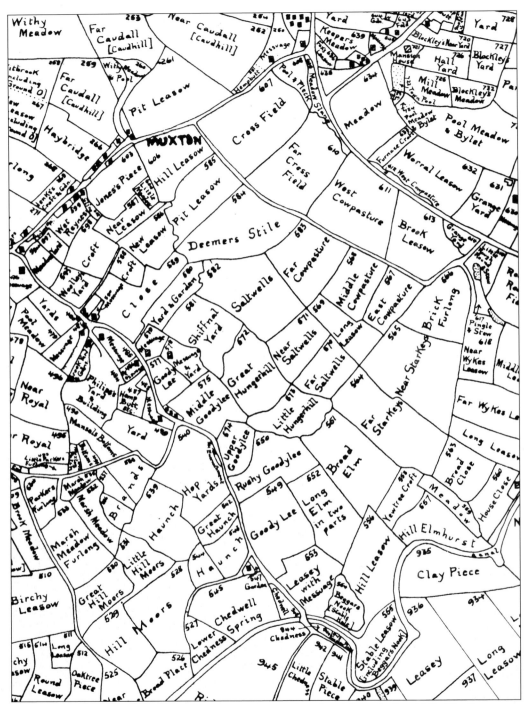

Tithe map of Muxton and the immediate area, extending southwards to Muxtonbridge, 1813. The Donnington Wood Canal winds across the bottom. Historically, land regarded as belonging to Muxton was limited to that on either side of Muxton Lane.

124

Some individuals did not appear to be farmers or labourers. Edward Aston (died 1708) was employed as a lime man, probably at Lilleshall Quarry. Another, William Cartwright, was a mathematician and died, in 1718, leaving various instruments and, unusually, 100 books. He was employed by the Leveson family as an agent and surveyor for mapping out their Lilleshall estate in 1679. One of his maps still survives (see p. 22). The ordinary labourers, of course, had very few possessions and undoubtedly led a hand-to-mouth existence. Their comfort would be dictated by the way they were treated by their yeoman employers. Some developed other skills; William Bate (died 1683) was a thatcher as well as a labourer and must have been busy replacing and repairing cottage roofs in the vicinity. Most buildings in the area had thatched roofs until the late eighteenth century.

It is obvious that Muxton was conspicuous by its relative insignificance, as most English villages are. It did not develop. It had no communal hall, no hostelry of its own (even in 1914, The Sutherland Arms was a Donnington property), no industrial heritage, no great variety in trades people. No important people took up residence there apart from Sidney Milbourne, Managing Director of C & W Walker's, who lived at Muxton Lodge until his retirement in the 1970s. In short, Muxton was something of a tranquil backwater. Even while industrial developments proceeded at an incredible pace during the eighteenth and nineteenth centuries, Muxton itself was, to all intents and purposes, ignored, although it does seem to have had a couple of small early coal pits in a field called Pit Leasow not far from the old main road. It was bound, of course, to benefit from activities along the Donnington Wood Canal and particularly from mining operations at Muxtonbridge Colliery (it can be argued either way that this mine fell within Muxton's territory but its existence is solely due to industrial developments in Donnington Wood) yet these benefits

Possibly the oldest dwelling in Muxton, c. 1910. It is unusual in that the earliest part of the building has an extended upper floor. Such timber framed cottages were often owned by yeoman farmers or folk who carried out a trade. Farm labourers frequently lived with their employers or rented a tied cottage.

125

The mission church of St John the Evangelist, c. 1960.

were confined to the sale of farm produce to a rising local population. Building activity, and hence a substantial increase in population, passed Muxton by. Until the twentieth century.

The Lilleshall parish church arranged for the mission church of St John the Evangelist to be erected around 1888 as a chapel of ease for the growing number of people living in and around Donnington rather than at Muxton. It cost the Duke of Sutherland a mere £100. Whereas nonconformist chapels tended to be built of brick, the mission church was made from corrugated iron, not only because it was considerably cheaper and the days of stone and brick built chapels of ease had largely been abandoned by the Church of England but also because it was deemed unlikely that there would be any requirement for a permanent church in this particular location. In some ways the parish church at Lilleshall had 'missed the boat' in much the same way as it had done in Donnington in the early nineteenth century. It had already lost considerable members of the congregation to the seemingly consistent and growing popularity of nonconformism and erecting the mission church could be regarded as acting a little too late. Nevertheless, it filled a spiritual gap at the time and provided seating for some sixty people, later reduced to forty-five when pews were installed. It was dismantled and sold to an anonymous buyer in 1998.

The parish boundary between Lilleshall and Donnington is marked by the course of a small brook which flows northwards from Muxton Marsh near the former Freehold mine. The brook crosses beneath the old Wellington-Newport road at Brookside, near what is now Muxton post office. Consequently, the vicar of St Matthew's parish church, Donnington Wood, whose vicarage was adjacent to the White House Hotel, actually resided in Lilleshall parish until a new vicarage was built in St Georges Road, Donnington Wood, during the 1980s.

Things have changed enormously since the beginning of the twentieth century. Semi-regular bus services to Wellington and Newport began during the 1920s. As a consequence, the few households there were in Muxton found it easier to visit these two towns for shopping and entertainment.

The first identifiable expansion of Muxton's frontiers appears to have taken place during the late 1950s when construction of Fieldhouse Drive (named after Field House, a Duke of Sutherland style building in Donnington) began. Houses at the far eastern end of the drive were in Muxton; the remainder were in Donnington. A few residents thought it was more up-market to say they lived in Muxton rather than Donnington and cited the parish boundary as also marking the western edge of Muxton. They were wrong: the parish boundary had no bearing on the matter; settlements often straddle such boundaries. However, streets laid down to the east of Muxton Lane (like Sutherland Drive and its offshoots) are definitely situated on land associated historically with Muxton.

Muxton's boundaries extended 'officially' during the 1990s when the Wrekin District Council declared that Muxton's western boundary should now be on the eastern side of Donnington Wood Way. Muxton's expansion is thus mainly the result of council intervention rather than demographic development. This has led to the odd situation whereby the majority of the original Donnington now lies within the current Muxton boundary, with its true historical origins seemingly disregarded.

Muxton Lodge, c. 1910. At that time it was occupied by R.J. Milbourne of C & W Walker Ltd.

A life size cast iron sculpture of a horse-drawn railway coal truck with an attendant collier, 1991. It was created in 1989 by G.J. Foxall of Tibberton and stood near the Old Lodge Furnaces. It has since been relocated to the middle of the Granville Roundabout at the northern end of Redhill Way.

Rustic symbols of Donnington's past. Timber-framed thatched cottages were usually occupied by yeoman farmers and farm workers. Those which survive probably date from the sixteenth century. These cottages, pictured around 1900, stood a few metres back from Wellington Road. The building on the right was, for a brief time, a public house.